Wealth

The Dream of Many, But a Friend of Few

Wealth

The Dream Of Many, But A Friend Of Few

An In-Depth Understanding of the Intricacies of Wealth Creation and Management

DERRICK KWAKYE

EXCELLER BOOKS™
A GLOBAL PRESS

ISBN: 978-81-19524-80-8

First published in India in 2024 by Exceller Books,
An imprint of GE Group

Address: G1, Dream Apartment, Degree College Road, Belgharia,
Kolkata, 700056, India

www.excellerbooks.com

Dedication

I dedicate this book to my wife Helena and my children Afia and Yaa for their understanding and cooperation to spare me time; otherwise, this book would have been delayed.

To my parents, aunts, and their husbands for their unwavering love and support.

To my pastors: Papa Darko and his wife, Israel, Edward, and Boakye.

To my friends who have become like family — Priscilla, Albert, Julie, Omari, Ben, Kofi, etc.

To my siblings, cousins, nephews, and nieces.

To all my readers.

Acknowledgements

In the deepest corners of my heart, I find solace in believing that there is God, and under His providence, love, and care, I was able to put this masterpiece together. It is the whisper in the wind, the warmth of the sun, and the spark of inspiration that ignite our souls. In this sacred dance of life, I bow my head and offer my humble gratitude to God.

I would also like to take this opportunity to express my heartfelt appreciation to all those who have contributed to the successful completion of this book. Their unwavering support, guidance and encouragement have played a pivotal role in making this book a reality. I would like to extend my gratitude to all the people through whom I developed the desire to write the book and to wealth management experts for their valuable insights and advice.

I would like to thank everyone I have come into contact with throughout the years. Without you, I would not be penning these words right now. Some of you have remained in touch with me, while others have had a significant impact on my life.

I also want to thank the editing and publishing teams for the wonderful work done on this book.

Finally, I want to offer my indefatigable gratitude to my wife and the kids, all my pastors, parents, siblings, aunts, best friends, and loved ones for their constant support, understanding, and motivation. Their confidence in my abilities and frequent encouragement has been crucial in helping me overcome obstacles and stay focused on writing this book.

Introduction

Allow me to introduce to you *"WEALTH: THE DREAM OF MANY, BUT A FRIEND OF FEW,"* a book designed to help you understand wealth and how it is generated. It will also assist you in making informed decisions about using assets, liabilities, income, and expenditures to generate sustainable wealth.

Many people have wondered why the rich keep getting richer, whereas the poor keep getting poorer. They often ask, is it true that some people are born wealthy while others are not? When and how may we get wealthy? The truth is that many of the wealthy people we see and hear about today did not come from wealthy families. They were once like many others who are struggling financially now. Some were even school dropouts, some could hardly afford three square meals a day, some were mocked, some cried for riches, and some were homeless.

If some of these wealthy people were previously nobodies and struggled like many others, what caused their financial condition to improve? This question can be correctly answered with the words of Jesus to the Jews in **John 8:32 –** *"And ye shall know the truth, and the truth shall make you free."*

Many people we see and hear about today and in the past have become wealthy after discovering the truth. The truth is that no one can become a medical doctor without first studying medicine. Similarly, a person cannot become an accountant without first studying accounting or a lawyer without first studying law.

Similarly, without a thorough understanding of wealth, it will be extremely difficult for a person to become wealthy and sustain their wealth. Unfortunately, wealth is the desire of many people, but it is not taught in our schools, homes, or churches. Only those who are prepared to be guided and invest resources in getting the essential information can learn more and become "friends" of wealth.

The book of **Mathew 7:7-8** says:
"Ask, and it will be given to you; seek, and you will find; knock, and it will be opened to you.
8 – For everyone who asks receives, and he who seeks finds, and to him who knocks it will be opened."

Many people today are too proud to ask about what they do not know, which leads to needless financial mistakes. Others have an erroneous notion that they must acquire more money before engaging in any significant activity or following their aspirations. Meanwhile, **Julia Abigail Fletcher Carney** described it brilliantly in her renowned poem **"Little Things."** *She said that little drops of water, little grains of sand, make the mighty ocean and the pleasant land.* You don't have to wait till you have more capital to start something.

You can start with a small amount of money and work your way up to a larger sum than you anticipated. Those who are anxiously seeking a dependable book to serve as a guide while making wealth decisions are frequently confronted with the difficulty of selecting the correct manual and, as a consequence, find themselves in an undesirable situation.

The Bible says in **Hosea 4:6:** *"My people are destroyed for lack of knowledge: because thou hast rejected knowledge."* This stunning verse underlines the value of knowledge and insight. When people lack knowledge, they are susceptible to destruction.

God blessed many individuals with finances and resources, but due to a lack of knowledge about resource management, they spent it and returned to zero.

Wealth is analogous to people who expect to be treated with care and respect and as valuable assets. If you do not take care of it, it will fall out of your grip and go to the next person who understands its worth and knows how to retain and multiply it.

This book provides a fresh perspective on wealth and its creation. It challenges prevailing notions and encourages readers to rethink their perceptions of wealth. By doing so, it aims to equip them with the knowledge necessary to navigate the intricate landscape of wealth creation effectively.

Whether you are a student of economics, an aspiring entrepreneur, a seasoned business professional, or simply someone interested in understanding wealth better, this book has something to offer. It is a practical guide that can help shape your strategies for wealth creation and management. An in-depth understanding of wealth is a thought-provoking exploration into one of the most critical aspects of our lives. It invites you to delve deeper, question more, and, ultimately, enrich your understanding of wealth.

After reading this book, you will undoubtedly be guided, enlightened and transformed in your journey to the "city" of wealth and learn how to use various assets, liabilities, income, and expenditures, thoroughly examined in this book, to build wealth.

Contents

Chapter 1:
Wealth Creation Concept

Wealth is not merely a concept; it is a tangible, quantifiable entity that can significantly enhance your quality of life. However, to fully grasp its importance, we must first define what wealth creation truly means. Wealth creation means simply increasing the value of assets, investments, and resources by you or your business over a period of time.

Wealth creation entails strategic planning, decision-making, risk-taking, long-term investment, compounding and early career investments. It also entails discovering new ideas and profitable prospects that are consistent with your financial goals.

At the most basic level, wealth creation is just about growing one's money or resources to achieve various short, medium, and long-term financial goals.

Furthermore, wealth is also about using one's resources, skills, knowledge and talents to make a positive impact on the world. This altruistic aspect of wealth is often overlooked, but it is equally important. The wealthiest individuals are not those who hoard their resources but those who use them to uplift others and make a difference in their communities.

Wealth is also about freedom—the freedom to make choices, pursue your passions, and live on your own terms. It is about having the financial stability to pursue your dreams without being constrained by the fear of financial insecurity. This aspect of wealth is perhaps the most liberating, as it allows one to live a life of fulfilment and purpose.

However, wealth is relative, and your level of wealth will be contingent on your goals and desires. You are in the right direction if you have sufficient resources to reach your financial objectives.

The common formula for determining wealth is **assets–liabilities**. However, for a better understanding of the key components of wealth and how they affect your wealth, I have modified the wealth formula.

Wealth is, therefore, calculated by adding the total market value of all physical and intangible assets owned to all income or gains and then deducting all liabilities and expenses incurred.

The wealth equation is modified as follows:

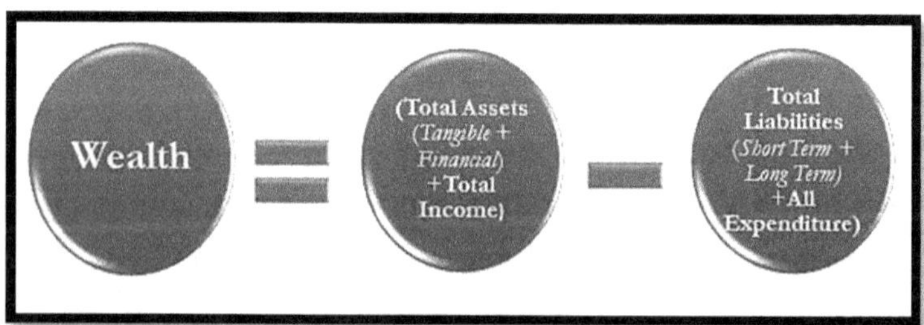

Figure 1.1

***Wealth= (Total Assets** (Tangible + Financial) **+Total Income) –
(Total Liabilities** (Short Term + Long Term) **+All Expenditure)***

It is necessary to note that each of the components in the above equation has a major impact on your net wealth. As a result, you must be circumspect when making decisions about them. To help you understand how the above equation works, a chapter has been dedicated to the key components of wealth. Take your time and read them; they will be extremely valuable to you.

❖ *Importance of Wealth Creation*
➢ *Future Financial Security*

Wealth creation is crucial for securing one's future through effective retirement planning and ensuring regular income to meet their personal and family needs.

Wealth creation fosters financial independence by providing a safety net during emergencies and allowing one to live freely.

➢ *Timely Meeting of Financial Goals*

Wealth building is critical for attaining long-term financial objectives like retirement planning, education financing and legacy planning. Investing early and consistently can help one build a substantial nest egg that can be utilized to fund future endeavors.

Systematic wealth creation enables timely financial goals by investing in diverse options suitable for short-term to long-term horizons, aligning them with respective financial objectives.

➢ *Promoting Economic Growth*

Wealth creation drives economic growth through job creation, increased consumer spending and business profits, creating a collective environment of increased investment opportunities for all investors.

➢ *Legacy for Future Generations*

Wealth creation enables one to create assets and resources for future generations, forming a legacy that safeguards their financial future.

➢ *Decreased Reliance on Debt*

Accumulating wealth reduces one's reliance on loans for various purposes, like home purchases, education, and business start-ups, as having one's own resources minimizes borrowing.

❖ *Essential Traits for Wealth Creation*

- **Vision:** Without a clear vision, generating substantial wealth will be very challenging. Your long-term financial goals serve as your vision, providing you with a sense of purpose and direction while you create wealth.
- **Passion:** Passion is an intense feeling of enthusiasm or excitement for doing something. Passion is a powerful driving force that can lead to wealth creation. When harnessed effectively, it can propel you toward financial success.

- **Skills:** Success requires skill in various aspects, including wealth creation, which allows individuals to control their financial future and build generational wealth.
Skills for wealth creation, covered in subsequent chapters, include the following:
  - ✓ Financial literacy
  - ✓ Entrepreneurial skills
  - ✓ Planning and decision-making skills
  - ✓ Investment management skills
  - ✓ Time management skills
  - ✓ Risk management skills
  - ✓ Debt management skills
  - ✓ Wealth preservation skills, etc.
- **Hard Work:** Building sustainable wealth requires hard work and a willingness to work at your own pace without succumbing to unnecessary pressures.
- **Resilience and Perseverance:** Wealth creation requires resilience, enduring financial setbacks, and learning from experiences. You need to persevere and grow stronger through learning from failures and disappointments.
- **Self-Discipline:** Discipline is one of the most important traits for successful and sustainable wealth creation. It is crucial for you to prevent impulse spending motivated by short-term rewards. Instead, implementing a disciplined strategy based on extensive research and analysis is essential for successful wealth creation.

- **Creativity and Innovation:** Individuals with a natural entrepreneurial spirit are able to identify opportunities and create unique value propositions, highlighting the importance of creativity and innovation in wealth creation.
- **Expertise:** To achieve successful wealth creation, one must gain experience in wealth generation processes, understand various investment vehicles, and utilize reliable information effectively.
- **Positive Mindset:** Wealth creation necessitates a positive mindset since it allows you to put in the necessary effort to reach your goals. A positive mindset will help you overcome discouragement from critics and shallow thinkers.
- **Commitment and Impulse Control:** To accumulate wealth, you need to prioritize long-term goals over instant gratification, live below your means and avoid impulsive spending.
- **Action-taking:** Wealth creation involves taking necessary steps, making prudent decisions, and stepping out of one's comfort zone, not just fantasizing.
- **Learning:** To be able to create wealth, one has to stay informed, adjust to changing circumstances, and keep up with the latest developments in personal finance, investment, and wealth-creation techniques.
- **Patience:** Patience is very crucial for wealth creation and asset growth. Wealth creation is a gradual

process that requires a lot of patience. You need to aim for steady progress and make prudent investment choices.

- **Entrepreneurial Mindset:** Adopting an entrepreneurial mindset can help one find opportunities and thrive financially. It promotes creativity, problem-solving skills, and market awareness. Having this mindset will enable one to add value and build their desired wealth.

- **Risk Tolerance:** Wealth creation involves extensive risks, necessitating thorough risk analysis before investment decisions. It is crucial to be open to stepping out of your comfort zone.

- **Adaptability:** It is key for wealth creation, and as a result, one may have to adjust to market conditions, investment landscapes and new technologies. Embracing new skills and opportunities is also essential for staying relevant.

- **Accountability:** It helps monitor your financial progress and performance, which are necessary for growing your wealth.

- **Humility:** It is a crucial trait in wealth creation, as it facilitates financial opportunities and promotes healthy relationships.

- **Emotional Intelligence:** It is important for wealth creation success because it allows for rational decision-making based on good analysis and emotional self-control, as well as preventing fear and anger from clouding poor decisions.

- **Character:** Wealth creation requires a comprehensive strategy that integrates financial knowledge with character traits to ensure long-term prosperity.

Chapter 2|
Objectives of Wealth Creation

The question that I usually ask is: Why do all of us work so hard? And why do some people cheat on others? Also, why do we have so many social vices in our world today? The answer is very simple: Every one of us is working so hard and doing what we need to do because we want to have a better and more comfortable life for ourselves and our loved ones. Thus, some use legitimate means to achieve the luxury or lifestyle they have always desired, while others use illegitimate means to achieve their needs. Wealth is also required to positively impact our community by making charitable donations, supporting small businesses, and investing in socially responsible projects that make society a better place.

In view of the above, we can say that one of the reasons why many people pursue wealth is to acquire a lot to meet their daily necessities of life and to be comfortable and financially independent.

The objectives of wealth creation can be summarized by a statement made by renowned investor Warren Buffet:

"If you don't find a way to make money while you sleep, you will have to work till you die."

He wanted to say that one of the primary goals of wealth creation is your ability to produce wealth passively by investing previously earned money.

Savings rise over time, increasing the investor's wealth. Also, one of the major objectives of wealth creation is to preserve your financial future and that of your family. You can acquire significant assets and develop income prospects as part of wealth creation to ensure financial stability even in the event of any unanticipated tragedy. This wealth can be used to cover unexpected financial emergencies or needs.

The objective of wealth creation is to increase your resources to achieve various short-, medium-, and long-term financial goals. Short-term financial goals could mean saving enough money for your wedding or renting an apartment. These are typically goals that need to be achieved within a period of 1 year.

Medium-term goals are usually investment goals that must be achieved within 1 to 5 years. Examples of such wealth creation goals can include saving for land, a new truck, or a down payment for a new house.

On the other hand, long-term goals, such as ensuring sufficient retirement savings and resources that you can pass on to future generations as part of your legacy or inheritance, can easily have an investment horizon that requires the longest time to invest, which is around more than 5 years and even decades. In this case, you need to ensure that you create enough wealth during your working life to support your post-retirement financial needs or legacy.

Chapter 3|
Financial Literacy

Financial literacy is essentially about acquiring sufficient knowledge, skills, and an understanding of finances and various investment portfolios, as well as how to evaluate and analyze them for decision-making purposes, ultimately achieving individual financial well-being.

The Organization for Economic Co-operation and Development (OECD) has defined financial literacy as "a combination of awareness, knowledge, skills, attitude, and behaviors necessary to make sound financial decisions and ultimately achieve individual financial well-being."

Financial literacy can also be referred to as **financial education**, **capability** and **awareness**.

It is crucial for you to understand that working hard to earn money is excellent, but what is more crucial is how you manage and utilize the money that you earn. You cannot effectively manage and utilize your money until you become financially literate.

Figure 3.1

It is important to emphasize that many people are in their current condition not because they did not have the opportunity or could not make money but because they did not have enough financial education.

You can make a lot of avoidable financial mistakes if you do not take the time to learn everything about finances and investing portfolios. Money is a crucial item in our lives, so we must pay close attention to it. People are willing to pay large sums of money to study a variety of subjects, but they have never considered paying money to attend financial and investment seminars and training.

Financial literacy programs sponsored by churches, schools, or associations often fail to reach many individuals due to their lack of awareness about its importance in their lives.

Many people have never asked important questions about wealth in their lives, but they are still going after it. How can you look for someone you do not know anything about? How can you become a friend of wealth if you have never sought to learn more about it? Financial literacy equips you with the knowledge necessary to manage your personal finances, investment portfolios and tax planning. Its major goal is to protect you against financial mistakes, fraud and scams.

You might use different excuses for not being well-informed about wealth and finances, but keep in mind that the consequences and costs of financial mistakes far outweigh the expense of attending wealth and financial seminars. Fortunately, there is what I call the "**The University of Social Media,**" which is a universal platform that contains a wealth of free educational resources and videos on any subject you care to learn about. You can start exploring the financial education available on these social media platforms. To discover more about personal finance, check **YouTube** or **Google Search**.

There are professionals in every field, including wealth management and finance. Before making any decisions about investments, loans, savings, or financial agreements, I recommend that you seek guidance from a financial consultant. This can assist you in identifying hidden clauses that can have a devastating impact on your wealth or financial situation.

It is also crucial to note that you can hire financial experts or consultants to help you manage your finances, assets, or wealth. You may be financially literate, but owing to your work schedule, it is recommended to delegate your financial resource management to a financial expert so that you can focus on your business or other equally important tasks. Remember that you cannot accomplish everything on your own. Therefore, it is better to invest a small portion of your budget in expert assistance than to lose it all.

Many wealthy people understand the value of contracting financial experts to manage their finances and investments, but unfortunately, the same cannot be true for the average person. You can improve your financial literacy by reading books about wealth and finance, such as the one you are currently reading. You can also listen to wealth management podcasts and videos, subscribe to financial information, attend seminars and conferences, or consult a financial professional.

❖ *The Importance of Financial Literacy*

- It is important for the realization of your long-term goals.
- Financial literacy equips you with the necessary skills to manage your personal finances and investments.
- It provides you with budgeting skills that are essential for decisions about financial resources.
- Financial literacy helps you know how to prepare for retirement, manage debt, and keep track of personal expenses.
- Financial literacy is essential to a prosperous financial future.
- Financial literacy helps you understand the key financial products you may need throughout your life, including bank accounts, mortgages, retirement

savings plans and basic investments like stocks, bonds and mutual funds.

- Financial literacy can help you avoid becoming the victim of fraud or Ponzi schemes.
- It helps you to know how to keep proper records of financial transactions so that you can manage your income and expenses wisely.
- Financial literacy is a crucial skill that enables you to make informed financial decisions and effectively manage your money.
- Financial literacy can help you with strategies for managing financial and economic risks effectively.

❖ *Key Components of Financial Literacy*

To become financially literate, you must first learn and comprehend the essential components of financial literacy, which are provided below. In the following chapters, I delved into greater detail about each of these components. Make time to read about them.

- Basic numeracy skills
- Understanding financial products and services
- Budgeting and money management
- Debt management
- Saving and investing
- Retirement planning
- Insurance coverage
- Risk management

❖ *Important Education on Secure Banking Practices (Information source: www.bog.gov.gh)*

- Your financial institution will not ask for any sensitive personal information, such as passwords and PINs, through phone calls, SMS or emails. Always authenticate the identity of a caller claiming to be a representative of your bank. Contact your bank when in doubt.

- The information on your card can be used by criminals or fraudsters for transactions without your approval, even if your PIN is unknown.

- Do not sign a blank cheque for a staff of a financial institution or any person for immediate or later withdrawal.

- Prevent the theft of your identity at the banking halls or elsewhere by properly disposing of all documents containing personal data such as name, account number, contact information, signature, etc.

- Beware of funds you receive in your bank account for yourself or on behalf of other persons, as this may be subject to anti-money laundering and countering terrorism financing laws. Always ensure the source of funds received in your account is legitimate. Do not allow anyone to use your bank account for a transaction. You are responsible for the activities on your bank account. Contact your bank when in doubt.

- Regularly monitor your bank transactions and account balances and report any unlawful, unauthorized, or suspicious transactions on your account to the institution. Contact your bank when you detect unauthorized transactions.

- Like the keys to your homes, your banking application login credentials, such as passwords, usernames and one-time passwords (OTPs), are highly sensitive and important assets in the digital world. Hence, properly secure them and contact your bank in case of any issues.

- Have you been unfairly treated by an institution licensed by your central bank? Report to the institution and, if not satisfied, report to your central bank for prompt redress.

- Demand to see a valid license from any one of the banking institutions and ask for a list of their permitted activities. Contact your central bank when in doubt.

Chapter 4|
Key Components of Wealth

It is important to understand the key components of wealth and how they influence your fortune. It should be noted that every decision regarding these components might have a positive or negative impact on your overall wealth. If you are aiming to build your fortune, then you must always assess whether the move or step you take will add value to your wealth.

If the response is yes, it is worthwhile; if the answer is no, the decision is bad and must be reconsidered. Let's take a look at the *KEY COMPONENTS OF WEALTH*, their meanings, types, examples, and how they affect your overall wealth.

The key components of wealth are:

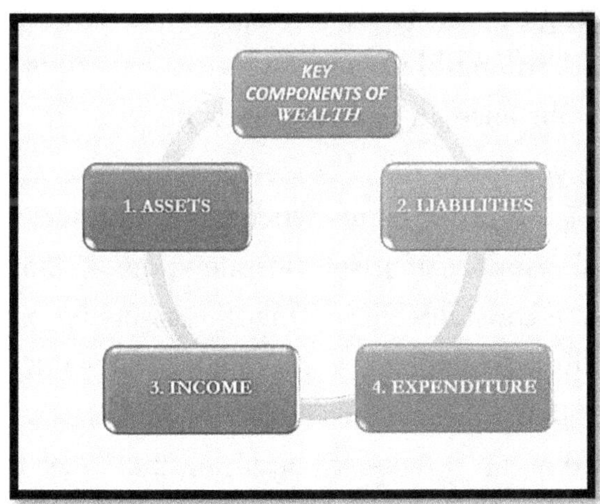

Figure 4.1

➢ *Assets*

An asset is a resource or possession with economic value that an individual or entity owns or controls with the expectation that it will provide future benefits. **Tangible (Physical) and intangible (Financial assets)** are two types of assets that a company or an individual can own.

Figure 4.2

Tangible assets are physical assets that can be seen or touched. **Intangible/Financial assets are** assets that lack physical substance. In general, assets boost your wealth by providing income.

On the other hand, when you continue investing additional resources in assets despite knowing that they do not provide considerable income, the assets become like a bad liability that depletes your wealth. In wealth creation, anything that delivers resources or income to you is considered an asset, whereas anything that takes resources away from you without a corresponding future income is considered a liability.

To increase wealth, it is critical to remember that the assets obtained must be put to the best use in terms of creating consistent income for you. If you are a beginner, you should avoid investing in assets that will not generate income for you and will instead drain a large portion of your finances.

The **"SHOW-OFF ATTITUDE"** has caused many people to be financially unstable. A person with a *"show-off attitude"* is someone who is not financially independent but uses all of their resources to construct a large building with many rooms to communicate that they, too, have made it in life. Sooner or later, the individual begins to struggle with finances and finds it difficult to maintain or retain the building. Instead of this massive structure, the individual could have invested these resources in their businesses or put up rented apartments to increase their fortune and gradually become financially prosperous.

Building assets simply means expanding your money or access to money through the purchase of assets. This is accomplished by acquiring assets that have current or future monetary value.

In general, acquiring more assets increases your net worth. This is only true if you have a lot more assets than liabilities or debt. So, when acquiring assets, it is important to limit the amount of debt you utilize and retain.

When it comes to asset creation, each step builds on the other. For example, money is required to purchase land and build a home. You can also leverage one to get another.

For example, you can sell shares in a company to fund a land acquisition. It is important to grasp this since asset building requires time and planning.

There is much more to asset building than merely increasing your net worth. Gaining access to money allows you to raise your standard of living and possibly accumulate wealth that will last for future generations.

What would you be able to accomplish with additional funds? You may start a business, put money aside for emergencies, or even pay for your child's college education. Having assets makes life easier and gives you access to more opportunities.

Finally, it is important to emphasize that while some assets lose value over time, others gain value. Investment portfolios, land and estates are a few examples of assets that appreciate in value. Automobiles, equipment, plants and machinery are examples of assets whose value depreciates. If you are an investor looking to grow your money, you should constantly concentrate more on making investments in assets that appreciate in value over time.

❖ *Examples of Intangible/Financial Assets*
- **Cash and Cash Equivalents** – Highly liquid assets, including actual cash or money held in bank accounts. Many people make the mistake of holding large amounts of cash in their bank accounts or

home savings boxes for an extended length of time without a plan. Though it is necessary to save, you must be aware of the **TIME VALUE OF MONEY CONCEPT**, which states that what **$1.00** may buy now may not be able to buy tomorrow due to **inflation** and **market fluctuations**.

It is, therefore, recommended that any cash that will not be used for several months be invested in a short-term interest-bearing investment portfolio, such as **a Treasury Bill** or **Fixed Deposits**. The goal is always to either increase or keep what you have while not getting worse off.

- **Accounts Receivable** – The amounts in an individual's or company's books that show the amount of money that is owed to the individual or company by its customers. If you are a business owner, it is crucial for you to **design debt recovery procedures** to avoid bad debts. Your inability to collect debts owed to you reduces your wealth.

  You should focus on selling to loyal consumers who pay promptly and without delay. **Short credit periods** can also be developed, and a demand for **bank guarantees can also be effective in reducing the risk of bad debt**. When it becomes increasingly difficult to collect debts from clients, **you may delegate the task to debt collection agencies, which employ a variety of techniques, including legal action, to collect debts.**

- **Patents** – A patent is the official legal right to make or sell an invention for a particular number of years. It is a type of intellectual property that gives its owner the legal right to exclude others from making, using, or selling an invention for a limited period of time.

  In most countries, patent rights fall under private law, and the patent holder must sue someone infringing on the patent to enforce their rights. It has the potential to increase the wealth of the owner.

- **Copyright** – It is the exclusive right that the owner of an intellectual property has to that property. It protects a creator's work from unauthorized duplication or use. It is the legal right to control the production and selling of a book, play, film, photograph, or piece of music. The owner's wealth increases when they sell their intellectual property, license it to others for money, or use it for marketing or advertising purposes.

- **Franchises** – A right to sell a company's products in a particular area using the company's name. A franchisor licenses some or all of its know-how, procedures, intellectual property, use of its business model, brand, and rights to sell its branded products and services to a franchisee.

  In return, the franchisee pays certain fees and agrees to comply with certain obligations typically set out in a franchise agreement. When the franchising agreement between the franchisor and the franchisee is finalized and the agreed-upon fee is paid, the owner's wealth increases.

- **Goodwill** – This is a part of a company's value that includes things that cannot be directly measured, such as its good reputation or its customers' loyalty trademarks and trade names (a name or symbol on a product that shows it was made by a particular company and that it cannot be used by other companies without permission). When a company is sold, goodwill is calculated as part of its worth. The additional monies realized boost the seller's fortune.

- **Any form of a digital asset** such as software or cryptocurrency, including stable coins and other financial instruments. A cryptocurrency, often known as crypto, is a digital currency designed to be used as a medium of exchange over a computer network, but at the moment, it is not supported or maintained by any central authority, such as a government or bank. Individual coin ownership is tracked in a computerized database that employs strong encryption to protect transaction records, manage the creation of new coins, and verify ownership transfers.

Figure 4.3

Cryptocurrencies are not considered to be currencies in the traditional sense, and they have received diverse legal treatments in various jurisdictions, including categorization as commodities, securities and currencies. Bitcoin is the most popular and valuable cryptocurrency. Whenever you diversify by investing in digital assets such as cryptocurrencies, you increase your wealth only if you make significant gains from the investments.

- **Financial Investments**

A financial investment is the setting aside of a certain amount of money with the hope of making gains from it. The goal is for the investment to grow or increase into a larger amount of money. The gains or the returns realized from the investment lead to an increase in your wealth. A detailed explanation of the various types of financial investments is provided below:

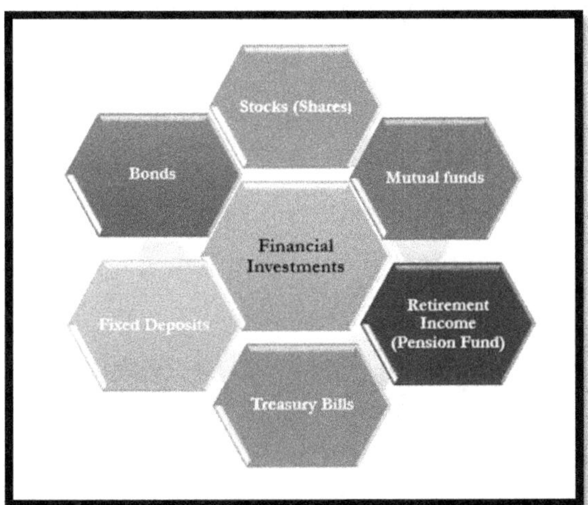

Figure 4.4

a) Stocks/Shares – They are fractional ownership rights in companies. They increase your wealth in two major ways. Firstly, your wealth is increased when a dividend is paid to you. Secondly, your wealth is increased when the price of the company shares appreciates. Shares are parts of a company's "ownership" that you pay for to earn the status of shareholders or stakeholders. You may have heard of investment lingo, such as equities and stocks, which are synonymous with shares (the most popular among startups). The purchase of company shares provides you with a percentage of everything owned by the company. It also allows you to participate in critical decision-making processes that may have an impact on the company, depending on the category to which you belong.

The two major categories of shares are *ordinary shares* and *preference shares*.

Ordinary shareholders have voting rights and bear the company's liability in the event of a winding-up, whereas **preference shareholders** typically do not have voting rights. However, they receive dividend payments before ordinary shareholders and have priority over ordinary shareholders if the company goes bankrupt and its assets are liquidated.

It is crucial to note that the fortunes of many affluent people around the world have expanded tremendously due to their numerous investments in various enterprises across multiple industries. As a person looking forward to developing wealth and achieving financial independence, you may not need to wait for big corporations to issue shares to the public before subscribing to them. You can simply hunt for a small, growing, and viable firm that needs additional capital to develop its operations and negotiate the purchase of a stake or share in the business in exchange for your funds. This means that you will receive a percentage of the company's yearly dividend when it is declared, as well as a percentage of the company's total net assets if it is sold.

b) Bonds – Bonds are investment securities in which you lend money to a corporation or government for a specified length of time in exchange for a steady stream of payments (*also known as interest payments or coupons*). This amount received (interest payments or coupons) is expressed as a percentage of the face value (the original money lent). At the end of the bond's tenure or lifetime, you then receive **100 percent of the bond's face value**.

On the other hand, there are some bonds that do not offer coupon or interest payments (**zero-coupon bonds**); these are priced at a discounted rate from their face value. When the bond reaches maturity or ends its lifetime, **the face value (original amount)** of the bond, along with the accumulated interest, will be received. Fixed income is a term commonly used to describe bonds, as your investment earns fixed payments over the bond's life.

Companies sell bonds to finance existing operations, new projects and acquisitions. Bonds are sold by governments to finance projects as well as to supplement revenue from taxes. When you invest in a bond, you become a debt holder for the entity that issued the bond. Many types of bonds, especially investment-grade bonds, are lower-risk investments than equities, making them a key component to a well-rounded investment portfolio. You can hold a bond until maturity or trade it on the secondary bond market.

Bonds are continually traded, and their capital value changes in line with interest rate movements and other economic factors. Traders of the bonds are large banks, brokers and broker-dealer institutions. These traders buy and sell bonds to profit from price fluctuations or generate coupon income. It is important to know that bonds have both a face value and a capital value. The face value is the amount you will receive back from the issuer when the bond matures at the end of a set term.

Most bonds make regular coupon (or interest) payments over the term of the bond. The capital value is what the bond is worth when it is bought and sold on the market. While the face value is fixed, the capital value can vary during the term, depending on factors such as interest rates and economic conditions. Bonds can help hedge the risk of more volatile investments like stocks, and they can provide a steady stream of income during your retirement years while preserving capital.

c) Mutual Funds – Mutual Funds (also known as unit funds) are made up of money pooled from multiple investors and are managed by professional investment managers to meet an investment objective. You own units (or shares) representing a part of the mutual fund's portfolio holdings. Mutual funds invest in stocks, bonds, or other securities according to each fund's objective.

While diversification is important in your investments, you will sometimes face the challenge of high minimum investment amounts when trying to do so across multiple asset classes.

Buying units in a mutual fund is an easy way to diversify your investments across various asset classes, geographies and strategies. This way, you will not have **'all your eggs in one basket'**. Also, most Mutual Funds offer daily subscriptions and redemptions, thereby providing regular access to your funds.

d) Fixed Deposits – It is an investment account that allows you to invest a lump sum of money for a specific period, usually ranging from **30 days to 365 days**. The interest rate on a fixed deposit account is fixed and higher than that of a savings account. Fixed deposit accounts are suitable for individuals who want to save money for a specific purpose or those who want to earn higher interest rates than savings accounts.

The interest rate on a fixed deposit account is determined by the amount invested, the duration of the deposit, and the bank's policies. Fixed deposit accounts offer several benefits and are known to provide higher interest rates than savings accounts.

The interest rate is fixed, which means you can predict your returns accurately. Furthermore, they provide an excellent opportunity to save money for a specific purpose, such as education, business, or retirement. Fixed deposit accounts also encourage disciplined saving, as the money invested should not be withdrawn until the maturity date. Withdrawals before the maturity date attract a penalty.

e) Treasury Bills – This is a form of borrowing by a national government for a period of time, usually up to one year, on which interest is paid at the end of the borrowing period. Treasury Bills are short-term debt instruments (securities) issued by the governments of many nations, and they have a maturity of less than one year.

They commonly have maturities of 91 days, 182 days and **364** days. Treasury Bills are issued at a discount from par, meaning that rather than making fixed interest payments like conventional bonds, income is earned by the difference between the face value and the security price. They are often considered risk-free as they are backed by the government's creditworthiness.

f) Retirement / Pension Fund – Retirement or pension fund refers to the process of allocating money for retirement into various asset classes. Pension funds are a form of mutual fund designed to make regular income payments to retirees.

Retirement income funds can be built around stocks, bonds, or a combination of the two and other assets such as private equity, real estate, or gold.

It   is   a system for saving money for   retirement. When the fund is well-managed, it generates interest or dividends, increasing your wealth in the long term.

❖ *Examples of Tangible Assets*

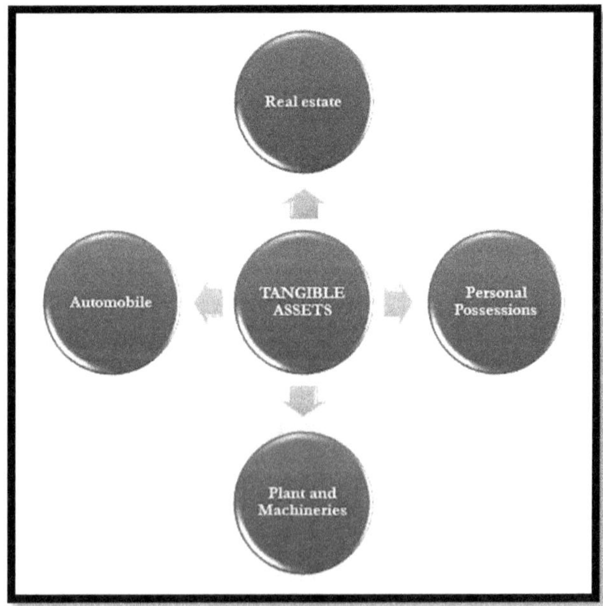

Figure 4.5

A. *Real Estate*

Real estate includes all homes, buildings and lands that are utilized for residential, commercial or industrial purposes. One of the best investments you can make is this one. A wonderful approach to ensure long-term financial security is by purchasing real estate.

Figure 4.6

Numerous factors must be considered when it comes to real estate, whether you are purchasing your first house or investing in rental properties. Before making any decisions, it is crucial to investigate the market conditions in the region you are considering and speak with experts like real estate agents or lawyers.

Dealing with contracts and discussions may be made easier by being familiar with the language and jargon used in the real estate industry. Overall, meticulous preparation is necessary when investing in real estate. Real estate includes both naturally occurring and man-made structures that are permanently affixed to or built on land. It differs from personal property, which is not permanently connected to the land, such as automobiles, boats, jewels, furniture and farm equipment.

Real estate investing in the world is less volatile than other options for business investment, such as stocks and mutual funds. It is still one of the safest investment alternatives in the world since it is a tangible asset. It is one of the most valuable tangible assets that will provide a consistent, steady stream of income to you for many years, even if you retire from active service or work. Unlike other investments, the value of real estate rises practically every day, enhancing your wealth.

✓ *Factors to Consider When Investing in Real Estate*

i. **Location**: When making an investment in real estate, one of the most crucial factors to take into account is the property's location. It might have an impact on real estate's market value and demand. Real estate in prime locations is probably more in demand and has a greater market value than properties in underdeveloped areas. A location near significant landmarks like roads, schools, marketplaces, retail shops, and hospitals is something you might want to think about.

ii. **Financing**: Identifying your financial capacity for real estate investments is crucial, as they often require full or upfront payment. Real estate purchase price is mostly fixed in a foreign currency like the US dollar. You can explore financing options like partnerships, equity funding and mortgages.

iii. Mortgages are the most common financing option when it comes to real estate investments. With the mortgage, you borrow money from a lender to finance the real estate acquisition and make monthly payments to defray the loan as agreed between you and the lender.

iv. Equity financing allows you to sell a portion of your stake in a company in exchange for investment funds, while partnership financing allows you to join hands with others to purchase real estate. It is always important to analyze the risks, payment terms, and benefits of the various financing options before making your final acquisition decision.

v. **Property Condition:** When investing in real estate, property condition is crucial since it influences market value, rental income and maintenance costs. In-depth examinations are required to identify any issues with the roofing, plumbing, electrical and foundation systems. Properly caring for real estate can minimize unexpected expenses and save you money, but some repairs may be necessary.

vi. **Market Trends:** The real estate market is continually changing and is impacted by variables such as interest rates, economic conditions, the rise in population and government regulation. Researching market trends in the area in which you have an interest is crucial for making informed investment decisions since high demand for rental properties may suggest a good investment opportunity.

vii. **Tax Implication:** Real estate investments provide tax advantages such as mortgage interest, property taxes and depreciation deductions. These deductions lower taxable income and enable you to invest the tax amount. Consulting a tax specialist is critical for identifying deductions and credits that maximize investment profitability.

viii. **Property Value**: It is also important to determine the worth of the real estate you intend to buy. This will allow you to select a financing option and assess the marketability of the real estate if you decide to sell it.

ix. **Expected Return on Investment**: You should also consider the prospective returns. This return can take the form of rental income if you choose to rent it out or a capital gain if you decide to sell it.

x. **Liquidity and Time Horizon**: You should also consider your liquidity needs and the duration of your investment. That is, if you decide to sell it in the future, how quickly can the real estate be purchased and the selling proceeds paid to you? The investment duration ought to be taken into account, particularly if it will be financed with a mortgage. It may take you longer to complete a mortgage payment, which may have an impact on your financial situation.

xi. **Property Type:** When investing in real estate, you need to know the type of property, whether it is residential, commercial, or industrial. Residential homes are less risky but may not yield as much income. Commercial properties provide better returns but carry greater risks, and success is dependent on tenant attitude. Industrial properties demand significant investment and management. You should examine the market to find the best return on investment.

xii. **Clauses in the Real Estate Contract**: You need sufficient knowledge about the real estate business in your country. You need to understand all the clauses in the real estate investment contract before going ahead. You also need to understand the procedure for acquiring the real estate in your country.

✓ *A Step-by-Step Guide for Real Estate Acquisition*

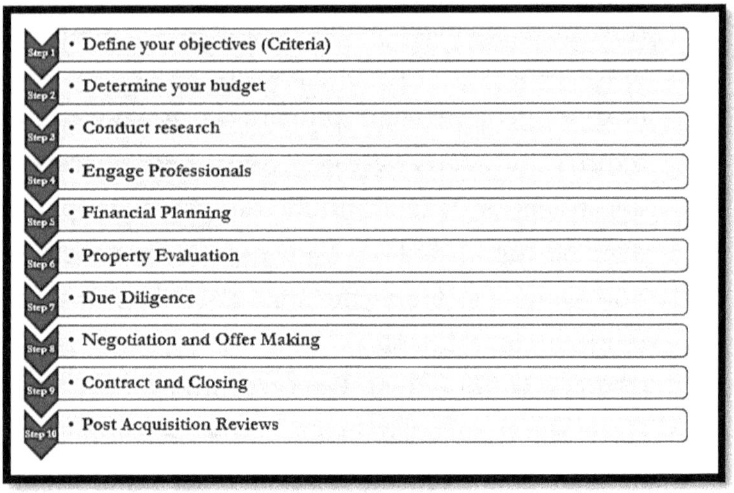

Step 1
• Define your objectives (Criteria)

Step 2
• Determine your budget

Step 3
• Conduct research

Step 4
• Engage Professionals

Step 5
• Financial Planning

Step 6
• Property Evaluation

Step 7
• Due Diligence

Step 8
• Negotiation and Offer Making

Step 9
• Contract and Closing

Step 10
• Post Acquisition Reviews

Figure 4.7

1) **Step 1: Define Your Objectives (Criteria):** First and foremost, determine your investment criteria. This will serve as a guideline during the acquisition process. Some things to take into account include the property's location, property type (residential, commercial, or industrial), demand and landmarks.

2) **Step 2: Determine Your Budget:** You need to know the maximum amount you can afford to pay for the property. Your budget determines the kind of real estate you get. The price of a 2-bedroom house is not the same as that of a 3-bedroom house, regardless of the location you consider.

3) **Step 3: Conduct Research:** It is crucial that you undertake extensive market research to identify the

numerous real estates for sale, their pricing, locations, and the terms and conditions offered by the respective property owners. To make an informed decision, you must have access to quality information. If you do not conduct significant market research, you risk being shortchanged.

4) **Step 4: Engage Professionals:** Hiring an investment expert to guide you through the purchasing process is essential if you are new to the real estate market. In their attempts to purchase real estate for themselves, many people have fallen victim to fraud. There are some terms and clauses that you might not comprehend. You will greatly benefit from the assistance of lawyers and financial advisors.

5) **Step 5: Financial Planning:** You have already determined your budget for the acquisition in step 2. It is good for you if you have the purchase price in your bank or investment account. If not, you may have to explore the financing options we have already discussed, such as mortgages, equity, or partnerships. You need to critically evaluate the terms and conditions offered under any of the financing options.

6) **Step 6: Property Evaluation:** Property evaluation involves the estimation of the price of real estate, taking into account factors such as location, size, property condition, prevailing market conditions and expected gain. At this stage, you must conduct

thorough inspections of the property you intend to buy.

You can estimate the property's value using two main methods: the sales method and the cost method. The sales method compares the price quoted for the property under consideration to the market value of similar properties in the same location, whereas the cost method attempts to calculate the cost of constructing the similar house you wish to buy.

7) **Step 7: Due Diligence:** Due diligence is crucial in real estate acquisition. This is where you do background investigations to determine the true owner of the property you want to purchase. You must conduct a search at the land registry or the government organization in charge of land or property registration. This will assist you in buying litigation-free land or property.

   The majority of real estate involves a leased agreement. You should find out how many years the land will be rented for, as you may have to renegotiate when the lease agreement expires. An outright purchase implies you own the land forever, and renegotiation may not be necessary in the future.

8) **Step 8: Negotiation and Offer Making:** At this stage, you have done all the searching, inspection, evaluation and due diligence. You are certain of the amount you want to pay for the property based on

your thorough evaluation. You now communicate your offer to the owner and negotiate the final price for payment.

9) **Step 9: Contract and Closing:** Once the purchase price has been agreed upon by the property owner and yourself, the next thing to do is review the purchase contract for signing. You must ensure you understand all the clauses and provisions in the contract before signing. The contract becomes legally binding immediately after it is signed. Get a lawyer or investment advisor if you need clarification or assistance before signing the contract.

10) **Step 10: Post Acquisition Reviews:** You have to keep monitoring the property if you acquired it through a mortgage and it is under the watch of a caretaker or tenant. You also have to keep a proper record of all your upfront and monthly installment payments to the lender.

B. Automobile

An automobile is a self-propelled motor vehicle intended for passenger transportation on land. It usually has four wheels and an internal combustion engine fueled most often by gasoline, a liquid petroleum product. It should be emphasized that electric vehicles were recently introduced to significantly reduce greenhouse gas emissions and contribute to a cleaner environment. The automobile is more commonly used as a car, formerly a motorcar; it is one of the most universal modern technologies manufactured by one of the world's largest industries.

It is crucial to understand that automobiles depreciate over time with regular repairs and maintenance. Investing in this automobile solely to satisfy your desire will result in no income. It will instead reduce your wealth. Keep in mind that if you purchase this vehicle for commercial purposes, you will increase your wealth through gains from the transport business.

If you intend to grow money and become financially independent, you should not buy a large number of cars for your garage without utilizing them. At the very most, you can get two for personal and family use and replace them when necessary.

C. Plant and Machineries

The term "plant" describes the whole infrastructure that a corporation uses. It includes a range of components required for industrial operations. Plant components include things like cranes, generators and boilers.

Plant refers more broadly to the tangible assets that support corporate operations. These resources support an organization's overall operation. Conversely, machinery particularly refers to the tools or mechanical devices that are employed for certain tasks. These devices carry out particular duties or operations. Lathes, drill presses and other specialized equipment used in building, manufacturing, and other industries are examples of machinery.

In conclusion, machinery concentrates on the particular equipment utilized inside the infrastructure, whereas plant covers the overall infrastructure. Both are essential to maintaining effective and secure operations across a range of industries. Similar to depreciating assets like cars, plants and machinery deteriorate over time. Buying them should be done with the intention of using them to generate revenue for you or your company.

D. Personal Possessions

Personal possessions include precious minerals, jewelry, art, collectables, etc. You can also invest in other tangible assets, such as minerals, through commercial banks or direct purchases from mining companies or license dealers. To purchase gold, inquire about the bank's or the dealer's physical gold offerings, compare their pricing to market and spot prices, purchase your gold option and obtain appropriate certificates. **The types of gold you can purchase are: coins, bars, ingots, and wafers.**

Note: It is crucial to emphasize that purchasing tangible assets may necessitate acquiring insurance coverage that protects against theft, fires and unanticipated disasters.

➢ *Liabilities*

Liabilities represent your debts or financial obligations. They typically require you to make payments or fulfill obligations over a specified period. It is a value that you or your business is expected to deliver in the future to satisfy a present obligation.

Figure 4.8

In general, liabilities reduce your wealth through future interest and principal payments only if they do not provide corresponding income or amount to you.

Furthermore, if you receive a loan or debt without investing it in a business or assets and default, it may have negative effects on your life and wealth, including business failure, harassment and property seizure. It is, therefore, recommended for you to be outside debt and not inside debt. **Being outside debt** means you borrow less than your total net assets value, and **being inside debt** means you borrow more than your total net assets value. In the context of wealth development, anything that deprives you of resources without providing equal income is called a liability.

To increase wealth, keep in mind that any loans or debts taken must be used to generate continuous income for you. Beginners, or people in general, should avoid liabilities or debts that will not generate money for them but will instead drain a large portion of their future finances or fortunes. As the scripture rightly put it in **Proverbs 22:7 – "The rich rules over the poor, and the borrower is the slave of the lender."** This verse emphasizes the importance of being responsible with our financial obligations. When you borrow money and fail to repay it, you become a slave to the lender, forfeiting your freedom and independence. Every type of liability or debt is intended to assist you in achieving your goals, and hence, they are not detrimental. However, what makes the difference is your due diligence prior to acceptance and how the funds were used. Globally, many people have lost their fortunes and even their freedom due to their inability to pay their debts. Numerous customers and even businesses were eager to accept loans without carefully reviewing the conditions and the terms that came with them. You may be aware that lenders expect to make profits rather than losses.

They will go to whatever length possible to recover the funds that were advanced to you, including all accrued interest. Because of the inherent risk, it is strongly advised to consult with a financial advisor before taking on any debt. There have been numerous cases where people were invited to come for loans and, without any consultation or thorough review of the terms, they collected the loans and spent them without using them for any business, resulting in their inability to pay, which has resulted in jail term and the loss of valuable assets. One of the things you have to understand when contracting a loan or debt is the interest rate. Interest rate is the amount that lenders charge you for the usage of their funds.

The **interest rates** charged by commercial banks in various countries vary due to the following factors:

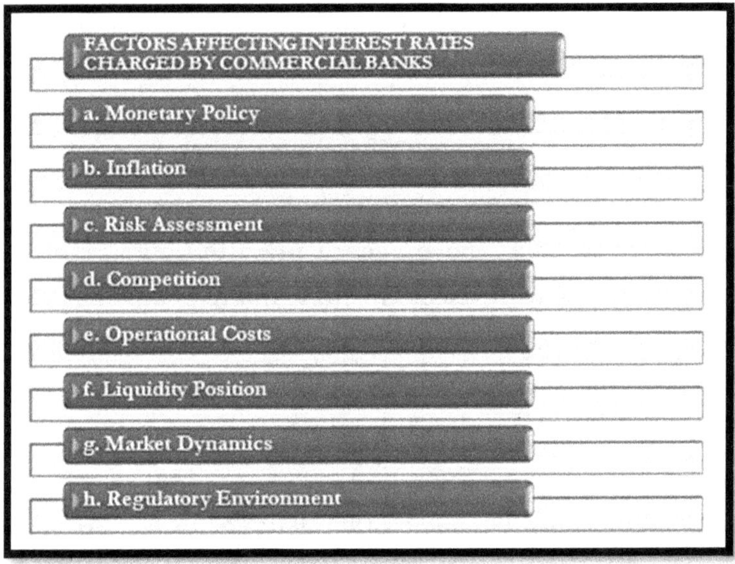

Figure 4.9

- **Monetary Policy** — The central banks determine the policy rate, which influences other interest rates in the economy and is used as a benchmark for commercial banks.
- **Inflation** — High inflation reduces the purchasing power of money. Banks consider inflation when determining interest rates. If inflation is significant,

banks may increase interest rates to compensate for the loss of real value over time.

- **Risk Assessment** – Banks evaluate borrowers' creditworthiness prior to issuing loans. Riskier borrowers (for example, those with a poor credit history) may experience higher interest rates. Different banks' risk tolerance thresholds vary, resulting in rate discrepancies.

- **Competition** – The banking sector is mostly competitive. Banks compete for clients by providing varying rates and terms. Some banks may opt to entice consumers by offering lower interest rates, while others prioritize profitability.

- **Operational Costs** — Banks incur operational costs, which determine the rates companies charge. Smaller banks may have a different cost structure than larger banks.

- **Liquidity Position** – The liquidity demands of banks have an impact on their lending rates. A bank with abundant funds may provide lower rates to lend out excess liquidity, whereas a bank with liquidity shortages may charge higher rates.

- **Market Dynamics** — External factors, such as global economic conditions, exchange rates, and commodity prices, influence interest rates. Nations' reliance on commodities, such as agricultural products and minerals, renders them susceptible to global market changes.

- **Regulatory Environment** – Banking regulations and prudential requirements established by the central bank also play an important role. Compliance expenses and capital requirements influence bank pricing decisions.

It is critical to understand the monthly interest rate before taking out a personal loan and to determine whether your budget can sustain the additional expense. However, it can be challenging to estimate the precise amount of interest before establishing a new loan.

There are two interest calculations commonly used in banking – **simple interest** and **compound interest**. When you are borrowing, make sure to read the loan agreement to understand how the interest will be computed on your balance and how often.

Let's analyze the two types of interest rates below:

❖ *Simple Interest*

With simple interest, the interest is paid only on the original amount, which is also called the principal. Simple interest is calculated by multiplying the stated interest rate by the principal by the number of years. When borrowing money with simple interest, as the principal is paid off, the interest is calculated on the remaining accumulated interest amount due. Simple interest loans are typically repaid in equal monthly installments. Part of each payment goes to payment of calculated interest due for the month, and the rest is applied to pay down the loan's principal balance.

Below is the formula for Simple Interest (SI):

Simple Interest (SI) = Principal × Rate × Time

Example: A customer borrowed $ 30,000.00 from the bank and agreed to repay it in 4 years with 15% interest. How much interest will he pay?

Solution:

Principal = $ 30,000.00, Rate = 15%, Time = 4 years.

Simple Interest = $ 30,000.00 * 15%*4 = **$ 18,000.00**.

With a principal of $30,000.00 and a rate of 15%, the customer will pay interest of **$18,000.00** under **the Simple interest method**.

❖ *Compound Interest*

Compound interest is slightly more involved when it comes to calculating the amount of interest paid. With compound interest, the interest earns interest. Each new interest payment is calculated on the original principal plus any accumulated interest. For a loan with compound interest, such as most credit cards, interest is added to the amount owed, and you pay interest on top of interest. The longer the loan balance sits unpaid, the more interest that accrues. If you keep a balance on a credit card, interest charges are added to the principal, which increases the debt exponentially over time. Today, the majority of formal interest payment calculations are compounded.

Below is the formula for Compound Interest (CI):

Compound Interest (CI) = Principal × (1 + Rate) ^Time - Principal

Example: A customer borrowed $ 30,000.00 from the bank and agreed to repay it in 4 years with 15% interest. How much interest will he pay?

Solution:

Principal = $ 30,000.00, Rate = 15%, Time = 4 years.

Compound Interest = (30,000.00(1+15%)^4)- 30,000.00

= (30,000.00 (1.15)^4)-30,000.00

= 30,000.00 (1.74900625)-30,000.00

= 52,470.19-30,000.00

= **$ 22,470.19**

With a principal of $30,000.00 and a rate of 15%, the customer will pay interest of **$22,470.19** under **the Compound Interest Method.**

In a situation where interest is compounded on a daily, monthly, or quarterly basis, the above compound interest formula will change to the below:

Compounding Interest = (Principal (1+Rate/number of compounding periods in one year) ^no. of compounding periods*Years) - Principal

Note:

- If the compounding is done quarterly, Number (no.) =4
- If the compounding is done monthly, Number (no.) =12
- If the compounding is done daily, Number (no.) =365

Example: A customer borrowed $ 30,000.00 from the bank and agreed to repay it in 4 years with 15% interest compounded monthly. How much interest will he pay?

Solution:

Principal = $ 30,000.00, Rate = 15%, Time = 4 years, Monthly Compounding = 12

Compounding Interest = (30,000.00(1+15%/12) ^12*4)-30,000.00

= (30,000.00(1+0.15/12) ^12*4)-30,000.00

= (30,000.00(1+0.0125) ^48)-30,000.00

= (30,000.00(1.0125) ^48)-30,000.00

= (30,000.00(1.8153548531)-30,000.00

=54,460.65-30,000.00

=$ 24,460.65

With a principal of **$ 30,000.00** and a rate of **15%**, the customer will pay interest of **$24,460.65** under **the Compound interest method.**

✓ *Examples of Liabilities*

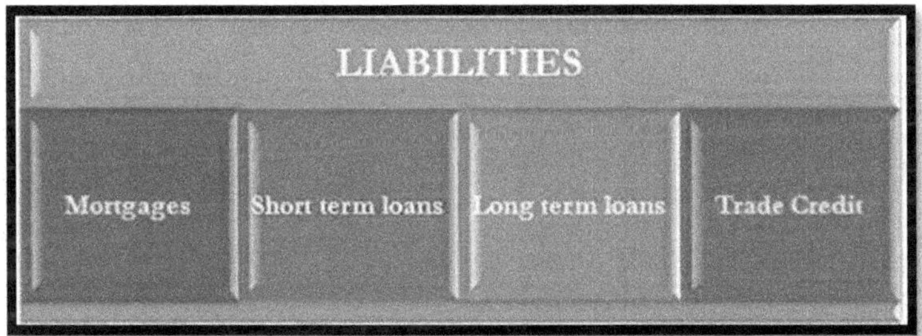

Figure 4.10

A. Mortgages

A mortgage is a special kind of loan where real estate serves as collateral. Essentially, the loan has a lien on the asset, meaning that the owner has the right to take the asset to pay off the obligation in a case of default on the part of the mortgagor. When you or your corporation takes out a mortgage, you are required by contract to repay the loan amount plus interest. However, in the case that the mortgage is not paid as agreed upon, the financial institution has a claim on the real estate property. Financial institutions will, in these cases, seek property foreclosure, allowing for your eviction and the property's sale.

The two parties may choose to have a **variable interest rate** or a **fixed interest rate** in the mortgage contract. Since interest is not paid up-front, the mortgage always forms an ordinary annuity.

1. **Under a fixed interest rate**, the principal is repaid in a number of equal payments that consist of both the interest and principal components of the loan. The interest amount is largest at the start and gradually decreases throughout the mortgage's amortization duration. Fixed interest rates in some nations are compounded annually or semi-annually; the latter is the more common option.

2. **In a variable interest rate mortgage**, the principal is repaid through an agreed-upon number of unequal payments that fluctuate with changes in borrowing rates. The principal and interest portions of the payment vary as interest rates fluctuate, implying that the interest portion can rise at any point with any increase in rates. When rates change, many financial institutions change the variable interest rate as of the first day of the next month.

- *Types of Mortgages*

The mortgage agreement may be open or closed. **An open mortgage** has few restrictions and allows the mortgagor to pay off the debt in full or make further prepayments at any time and in any amount without penalty. **A closed mortgage** contains numerous regulations that govern how the mortgage is to be paid. It prevents the mortgagor from paying off the obligation in full until the loan expires. **Most closed mortgages** include **"top-up"** options that allow the mortgagor to make additional payments (such as an additional 20% per year) on the mortgage without incurring penalties. Any payments exceeding the maximums or early repayment of the mortgage are severely penalized, with a three-month minimum interest charge that could be increased up to a measure called the interest rate differential, which effectively assesses the bank's loss and charges the mortgagor this full amount.

In conclusion, it is critical for you when seeking to expand your wealth to carefully assess your financial circumstances and comprehend the conditions, terms and modalities of the mortgage agreement before entering into it. Failure to comply with the terms and conditions of the mortgage agreement might have serious implications, reducing your wealth.

NB: A mortgagor is the **borrower of a mortgage loan** who is getting the loan to buy a home or real estate property. A mortgagee is the **lender of a mortgage loan,** who is providing the mortgage money and determining if the mortgagor qualifies for the loan. The mortgagor makes regular payments on the loan and agrees to a lien on the mortgaged property as collateral for the mortgagee.

B. Short-term Loans

A short-term loan typically refers to a loan that must be repaid within a relatively brief period, usually **within a few months to around a year**. These loans are often associated with your need for **quick access to a relatively small amount of money**. Short-term loans may not require collateral as in the case of long-term loans.

Examples of short-term loans include **cash advance loans** and loans obtained through **peer-to-peer lending**. The repayment period for short-term loans is relatively short, making them suitable for urgent financial needs.

Below are some of the examples of short-term loans:

i. Amounts owed on credit cards with interest charges.

ii. **Student Loans:** Loans taken to finance education and tuition fees.

iii. **Personal Loans**: Borrowed funds for personal use.

C. Long-term Loans

A long-term loan has a longer repayment duration, ranging from several years to many decades. These loans are often necessary for larger sums of money or transactions with major financial obligations. Long-term loans include purchasing vehicles, home purchases and other large-scale finance needs. The prolonged repayment period enables borrowers to manage larger payments over time. In conclusion, long-term loans are better suited for more major expenditures or expenses.

D. Trade Credit Facilities

Trade credit is a loan provided from one merchant to another or individuals when products and services are purchased on credit. Trade credit enables you to purchase supplies without immediate payment. Trade credit is a popular short-term funding option for businesses. It is granted to consumers with an acceptable level of financial standing and goodwill. Many businesses, especially SMEs, are being made to offer credit facilities to customers in a bid to encourage patronage. The mismanagement of this trade credit, however, can lead to a devastating plunge in the financial performance or wealth of the individual or business.

> ## *Income*

Income is the money you receive regularly, typically from employment, investments, or other sources. Income can also be a company's profit in a particular period of time. Under this component of wealth creation, we are more concerned about the monies that flow to us or our business, which, when properly managed, have the potential to improve our wealth.

The issue is not about how much income you earn but rather how the income received is utilized. Wealthy people are cautious about how they spend their money. The most important question they constantly ask is: how can this income generate additional income for me and my family? When the wealthy receive their income, they first set some aside for future investment before spending the rest. This should be the guiding principle for you if you are desirous of growing your wealth. People who are employed should focus on other areas where they can earn more money because there is the saying, **"Don't put all eggs in one basket."**

There are a variety of strategies you can employ to improve your income. Remember that your salary may depend on your employer, location and experience, so some methods may be more successful than others. Try to establish realistic expectations when pursuing more income. Additional income can also come from starting a new business, learning new skills, improving what you currently know or do, working extra hours, or taking on a part-time job.

It is the desire of God that people prosper, as enshrined in **3 John 1:2** when John says: "Beloved, I wish above all things that thou may prosper and be in health, even as thy soul prospers." It is important to remember that **success does not come easily and can never be achieved on a silver platter**. It reminds us that **true success requires effort, determination and resilience.** Similarly, making income is not about praying without acting, nor is it about being hopeful or fantasizing. However, it requires hard work and concentration.

The scripture encourages God's people to work hard and smartly for prosperity, as captured in the following verses:

- Proverbs 20:13 says: "Do not love sleep or you will grow poor; stay awake, and you will have food to spare."
- Proverbs 22:29 also says: "Do you see someone skilled in their work? They will serve before kings; they will not serve before officials of low rank."
- Proverbs 10:4 says: "He who has a slack hand becomes poor, but the hand of the diligent makes rich."

❖ *Types of Income*

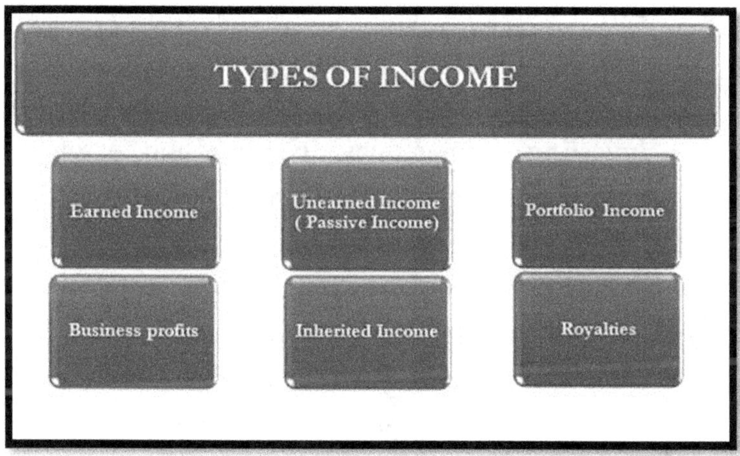

Figure 4.11

A. Earned Income

It is earned by **doing an active job** on a daily basis. This type of income is usually fixed and comes with a contract for a specific period of time in the form of salaries, wages, bonuses, allowances and commissions. Earned income is the most common type of income that most people receive.

B. *Unearned Income or Passive Income*

Passive income is the **money that is earned without having to actively work** on anything. Initial work paves the way toward earning passive income in the future. Passive income is usually not a fixed number but rather fluctuates every now and then. This is the best type of income for anyone as it allows you to earn money while you work on other tasks or businesses. *(You can earn passive income even while you are fast asleep).*

Below are examples of Passive incomes:

- **Rental Income:** Rental income refers to **income you earn by renting** rooms, houses, apartments or any type of shelter for living/storage purposes.
- **Dividends:** Dividend income is **earned by investing your money in** stocks and earning a percentage of money based on the amount of money you have invested in it. This type of income is earned when the company makes a profit and declares dividends for the period.
- **Interest:** Interest refers to any sort of **money you accumulate due to storing your money** elsewhere. For example, interest can be accumulated at the bank for placing your money at the bank for long periods of time. Interest can also be earned by lending money to someone else and collecting it

back with an additional amount of money, depending on how long they kept it.

- **Social Security/Pension Benefits:** Pension schemes provide benefits to retiring workers at their compulsory retirement age, varying across countries. Pension schemes aim to secure the future of workers upon retirement. I have carefully outlined the pension benefits that are paid to the people of Ghana upon retirement. Juxtapose it with what is paid in your country if you are not from Ghana.

The new National Pension Scheme was instituted by the National Pensions Act, Act 766, which ensures that every Ghanaian worker receives retirement benefits as and when due.

Act 766, which was passed on December 12th, 2008, mandated the establishment of a new contributory Three-Tier Pension Scheme with the National Pensions Regulatory Authority (NPRA) to oversee the efficient administration of the composite pension scheme.

The New Pension Scheme was launched on **16th September 2009**, and its implementation started in **January 2010.**

✓ *Contribution Rates and How They Are Distributed Between the Employer and Employee*

Worker – 5.5% of workers' basic salary

Employer – 13% of workers' basic salary

Total – 18.5% of workers' basic salary

Out of the **18.5%**, an employer remits **13.5%** to SSNIT within 14 days following the end of the month to the mandatory First-Tier Basic Social Security Scheme.

Again, out of the **13.5%** paid to SSNIT, **2.5%** is sent to the National Health Insurance Authority (NHIA) for the member's health insurance.

The residual **5%** is sent to the mandatory Second Tier Occupational Scheme which will be privately managed by Trustees approved and licensed by the Board of NPRA.

Ghana's pension system consists of three tiers:

- **Tier 1:** Mandatory basic national social security scheme: **The First Tier** is the Basic National Social Security Scheme for all workers in Ghana. It is a defined benefit scheme and mandatory for workers to have **13.5%** contributions made on their behalf. The contribution is managed by SSNIT.
- **Tier 2**: Mandatory fully funded and privately managed occupational pension scheme. **The Second Tier** is a defined contributory Occupational Pension Scheme mandatory for workers with a **5%** contribution made on behalf of members. The contribution is managed privately by approved Trustees.
- **Tier 3**: It is also called Provident Fund (PF). The Provident Fund Scheme is a **voluntary, fully-funded and privately managed pension scheme.** Its purpose is to provide employees with lump sum payments at the time of exit from their place of employment. This differs from pension funds,

which have elements of both lump sum and monthly pension payments. It is designed to offer both employers and employees the opportunity to make extra savings towards their retirement. Under this tax-privileged voluntary scheme, employees and employers can contribute up to **16.5% of their monthly basic salary**.

Members have the freedom to contribute to the scheme based on their financial capacity and retirement goals.

Also, contributions made by employees to the provident fund scheme are **exempted from tax** only if withdrawals are made after **10 years** of contribution. Currently, withdrawals from this fund before the **10 years** attract a withholding tax at the rate of **15%**.

C. Business Profits

Profit is an income that is usually earned by **buying** a product or service and **selling** it at a higher price. The difference is called the profit. This type of income is not fixed and generally depends on how many products or services you manage to sell.

D. Portfolio Income

Portfolio income refers to **profit earned by investing** in and selling stocks or assets at a profit after a period of time. It can also be referred to as capital gains. The gains derived depend on the performance of the securities markets.

E. Inherited Income

Inherited income is money that you receive from your family. It is usually passed down from generation to generation to fulfill their business activities and involve in other ventures. While this type of income is most common among wealthier families, inherited income does not always come in the form of money; it can also come in the form of an asset.

F. Royalties

A royalty is a **small percentage** (usually between 2% and 10%) **paid to** the creator, original owner, or **anyone involved in creating a product or service** long after they are created. They are paid whenever a sale goes through or their product or service has been used by their audience. Royalties are very common amongst movie stars, as they get paid royalties for their creations long after the release of the production.

In conclusion, your income is largely dependent on your assets and liabilities. As a result, they must be managed and utilized carefully.

Typically, the higher your income, the higher your net wealth. Or, better said, the higher your income, the higher potential you have for a higher net wealth.

> ➢ *Expenditure*

Expenditure is a payment made in cash or on credit to purchase goods or services. Expenditure is an important factor in shaping your wealth. Let's look at how expenditure affects wealth. When you feel wealthier as income or asset prices rise, you tend to spend more. For example, when your assets rise, you may raise your spending.

Many people nowadays struggle with the ability to discipline themselves and discern what they truly need rather than what they want. People either waste resources on items they already own and do not use, or they purchase items they later realize they do not really need. Many people rarely sit down and plan out how they want to spend their financial resources.

However, people have become accustomed to making impulsive purchases. Some people live their lives as if they are competing with others, and they want to buy practically everything they see in others, even if they do not need it. It is also true that some people are in their current circumstances not because God did not bless, favor, or provide them with numerous opportunities, but because they were not careful in handling the resources provided to them. Also, many people believe that they are young and have more years to live before retiring, so they spend their money irresponsibly without proper guidance.

It is also crucial to acknowledge that while some people are in a difficult situation due to no fault of their own, many people are still unaware that unforeseen circumstances might render them incapacitated and unproductive. We must recall **Proverbs 6:6-8.**

"Go to the ant, you sluggard! Consider her ways and be wise,
7 Which, having no captain, Overseer or ruler,

8 Provides her supplies in the summer, And gathers her food in the harvest."

This proverb promotes diligence, resourcefulness and preparation. The ant's diligence teaches us important lessons about self-discipline, preparedness and responsibility. Despite the lack of external authority, the ant tirelessly prepares for the future, gathering food in abundance to support itself in times of scarcity. In our personal lives, this proverb admonishes us to be proactive, work hard and prepare ahead. As the ant prepares for winter, we must prudently manage our resources and responsibilities, even without external supervision.

❖ *Categories of Expenditure*

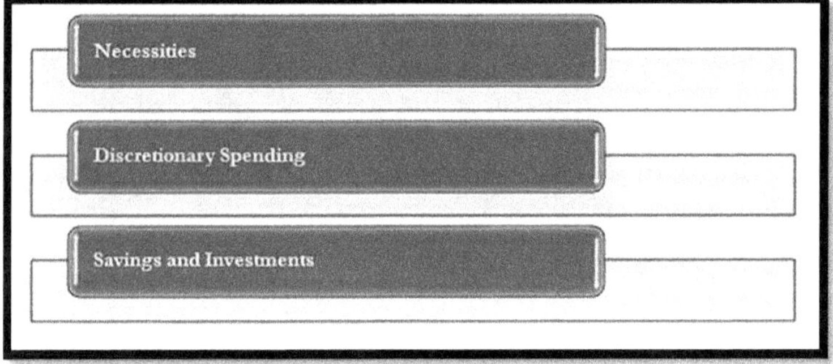

Figure 4.12

- **Necessities**: Fundamental requirements for human survival, such as housing, food, utilities, healthcare, etc. Necessities are needed for human survival, and people who want to build wealth must focus more on these necessities.

- **Discretionary Spending**: It refers to **optional spending that is not required**. It is often defined as non-essential spending. Examples of discretionary spending include dining out, shopping, entertainment, vacations and subscription services. Discretionary expenses are costs that a business or household can survive without, if necessary. People who are not financially independent must not waste their precious resources on these until they are financially prosperous.

- **Savings and Investments**: They refer to contributions to savings accounts, retirement funds, etc. Spending on these is worthwhile since they will produce future income, increasing your wealth. You can spend more on these.

- In conclusion, while expenditure can increase wealth through asset appreciation, it is critical to establish a balance. Focusing on wealth generation, preservation, and avoiding over-spending and over-borrowing are intelligent measures to sustain financial well-being.

Key Takeaway from Chapter 4

Remember, wealth is not just about the accumulation of assets; it also involves managing liabilities, optimizing income and making informed expenditure choices. Balancing these components contributes to overall financial well-being.

Chapter 5|
Processes of Creating Wealth

Creating wealth is a long and gradual process based on several essential factors. Individuals who are avidly pursuing abundant wealth must comprehend the processes of wealth creation. Every game has a technique or process that participants must follow in order to be successful, and the same applies to wealth creation. Study the processes outlined in this chapter carefully since they will considerably assist you on your path to wealth creation and financial freedom. The following are the processes for creating wealth:

- Goal-setting and plan-devising
- Earn money
- Budgeting
- Savings
- Investment
- Protection of assets
- Debt management
- Continuous financial education
- Strong supportive network
- Commitment to long-term goals

Now, let's take our time and delve deeper into the above-mentioned processes one after the other.

❖ *Goal-Setting and Plan Devising*

A goal is a vision of desired outcomes or achievements encompassing personal, professional, or life-related aspects. It is set to motivate, focus, and measure progress and guides actions and decisions in various aspects.

Goal-setting is an important step in generating wealth. When you have a clear picture of what you want to accomplish, you can devise a strategy to assist you get there. The first thing to do is to assess your financial condition to know how much you owe, how much money you have, and what your aspirations are. **"You can't get to where you want to go without knowing where you're starting from," said Sabatier.**

Define your financial goals clearly. Develop short- and long-term objectives that are specific, measurable, achievable, relevant and time-bound (**SMART GOALS**). Whether you are saving for retirement, buying a home, paying off debt, or establishing a business, clear goals will drive your wealth-building journey.

Once you have determined your goals, you should devise a plan to achieve them. A plan is a detailed diagram or list of steps with resources and timing for completing a task, consisting of scheduled actions to achieve a specific goal. This could include developing a budget to help you save more money, improving your income through education (training) or career advancement, or investing in enterprises or assets that will grow in value over time.

Your plan should be pragmatic, flexible, and long-term oriented. To stay on track, check your progress on a regular basis and make any necessary modifications.

❖ *Earn Money*

Money is any item that is used as a **medium of exchange** in transactions.

Figure 5.1

Money has traditionally been described as a unit of account, a store of value and a medium of exchange. Money can also be described as a **compensation** or **reward** for service. You can exchange your skills, labor, or goods for a universally accepted form of value. Money is an important part of our daily lives, whether it is a wage for a hard day's work, payment for a product, or a tip for great service.

Money is more than simply bits of paper. It functions as a medium of exchange, facilitating trade. Assume you have a phone and would like to swap it for a laptop without the use of money; you need to find someone who has a laptop to give away and happens to be looking for a phone. Obviously, this is going to be extremely challenging. This is referred to as the **"double coincidence of wants problem."** The good thing is that the introduction of money allows for a more flexible approach to trade than barter, which has the double coincidence of wants problem and is also referred to as **the dual coincidence of wants**.

The next step in the wealth creation process is to start making money. Whether through earned income (from your employment) or passive income (from investments portfolio), you need to generate income to save and invest. This step may seem apparent, but it is critical because you cannot save and invest what you do not have. You have probably read books or watched business programs demonstrating how a small amount of money saved on a regular basis and allowed to compound over time can eventually grow into a large sum. However, those books or business programs never address the most basic question: How can one generate money to save and invest in the first place?

There are two primary ways to get money: through **Earned or Active income and Passive income**. Earned income comes from the main job you do for a compensation or reward. It is a one-time income, whereas passive income comes from investment gains and price appreciation. You are unlikely to have any passive income until you have earned enough money to begin investing.

> ➤ *Differences between Earned Income and Passive Income*

No.	Diffentiating Factor	Earned Income	Passive Income
1	Time to Generate income	Time is invested	No Time is invested
2.	Effort / Active Involvement	Effort is Required	No Effort Required
3.	Frequency of Earning	Actively Working	Actively Investing
4.	Presence	One has to be present	No presence/one can sleep
5.	Participation of People	Majority	Minority
6.	Origination of Income	Employment/Business	Investments, real estate etc.
7.	Responsiveness of People	Likes/Positive	Dislikes /Negative
8.	Impact on Wealth	Minimal	Huge
9.	Categorization /Designation	Poor / wretched	Wealthy/Affluent
10.	Condition / Situation	Suffering/ Survival	Comfort/Abundance

Table 5.1

> ✓ *Explanation of the Above Table*

Earned income requires time and effort on your part. It also demands your actual presence to do and supervise the work. In contrast, passive income does not require your time, effort, or physical presence to generate revenue for you. You can just sleep while your money works for you.

In addition, you can only earn income when you actively work. Similarly, you can only get passive income if you actively invest. When you quit actively working and investing, there will be no earned or passive income.

It is also worth noting that the majority of people participate in earned income rather than passive income, maybe due to the inherent risks of the various investment vehicles used to generate passive income. Risk-averse people are always content with their jobs or businesses and will not like taking risks by investing in securities. People are generally more optimistic about earned income, but the opposite is true for passive income.

Furthermore, the impact of earned income on your wealth can be minimal compared to passive income, which can have a huge impact on your overall wealth.

Lastly, poor people who are at a survival level of wealth are the ones who participate a lot in earned income, while the comfortable wealthy participate in passive income.

When deciding on your career path, think about the below questions:

- **What do I enjoy doing?** Doing something you enjoy will improve your performance, lead to a longer-lasting career, and increase your chances of financial success.
- **What am I skilled at?** Consider what you are good at and how you may use those skills to get money.
- **What will pay well?** Consider occupations that allow you to do what you enjoy and are good at. The Occupational Overview or Industrial Journal is a valuable resource for wage statistics and future growth possibilities in a variety of areas.
- **How do I get there?** Learn about the education, training and experience requirements for your chosen career path.

➢ *Mediums for Generating Money*

There are numerous ways for individuals to create money to enhance their wealth. Unfortunately, many people rely solely on regular occupations and disregard other avenues for generating sufficient money. People constantly complain about a lack of jobs in their country and blame the government for their problems.

Some graduates go so far as to join an Unemployment Graduate Association rather than focusing on what they can achieve with the knowledge they have gained from their higher education.

Many people have also overlooked their God-given abilities, which could have made them wealthy, in favor of pursuing jobs that are difficult to come by. Unfortunately, many people who have been employed are either underutilizing their abilities or doing jobs that they are not supposed to do. Sadly, many people dislike skilled professions but have high regard for white-collar jobs (office jobs), and as a result, they would prefer to sit at home for an extended period of time rather than engage in any skilled activity.

It is time for us to change the narrative by exposing our children to skilled professions in addition to the education they get. This will assist many of them in discovering a niche even before they complete their studies.

The mediums for generating money are:

Work	Ideas	Problems
Opportunities	Gifts and Talents	Product & Services
Dreams & Visions	Partnership, Networks, Groups, People	Wisdom
	God (Creator)	

Figure 5.2

Now, let's do an in-depth analysis of the aforementioned mediums via which money can be generated:

A. Work

Making money from work entails utilizing your abilities, expertise, time, and effort to earn an income. You can either use your skills or expertise to work for yourself or others for compensation or reward.

Here are some ways to monetize your work:

- **Full-time Employment**: Work for a company or organization and receive a salary or wages.
- **Teaching or Coaching**: Share your expertise and teach others through online courses, workshops, or one-on-one coaching.

- **Creating and Selling Digital Products**: Develop eBooks, courses, software, or other digital products that showcase your talents.
- **Freelancing**: Offer your skills and services on a project-by-project basis to clients.
- **Consulting**: Provide expert advice and guidance to individuals or businesses.
- **Entrepreneurship**: Start your own business, creating products or services that generate revenue.
- **Selling Products Online**: Utilize e-commerce platforms like Amazon, Etsy, or eBay to sell products.
- **Renting out Assets**: Monetize underutilized assets, such as renting out a spare room.

B. Ideas

Making money from ideas requires creativity, innovation, and, in many cases, a willingness to take calculated risks. Many of today's inventions are the result of people's ideas. It is also crucial to note that people became affluent due to the ideas they received. Some sold their brilliant ideas for millions of dollars, while others turned them into profitable enterprises that they are still running today. Others made mistakes by sharing brilliant ideas with the wrong people, who then sold or used them. It is crucial for you to jot down your ideas as soon as they occur to you because you can easily forget them. Remember that making money from ideas needs dedication, hard work and a willingness to learn and adapt.

Here are some of the ways to monetize your ideas:

- **Start a business**: Turn your idea into a product or service that solves a problem or meets a need in the market.

- **License your idea**: Sell your idea to a company or individual who can develop and market it.

- **Create and sell digital products**: Write an eBook, develop a course, or design software that solves a problem or entertains.

- **Patent and sell your invention**: Protect your idea with a patent and sell it to a company or individual.

- **Create a mobile app or game**: Develop a popular app or game that generates revenue through in-app purchases or advertising.

- **Monetize your content:** Create a blog, YouTube channel, or social media presence and earn money through advertising, sponsorships and affiliate marketing.

- **Offer consulting or coaching services**: Share your expertise and help others achieve their goals.

- **Create an online course:** Share your knowledge and skills by creating an online course and selling it on platforms like Udemy, Teachable, or Skillshare.

- **Affiliate marketing**: Promote products or services of other companies and earn a commission for each sale made through your unique referral link.

- **Crowd-funding:** Use platforms like Kickstarter or Indiegogo to fund your idea and validate demand.

C. Problems

Making money from problems entails identifying solutions to specific pain spots or challenges. Identifying and resolving **worthwhile problems** is critical for those pursuing financial success. You might start by assessing the difficulties that people in your area are facing and the kind of solutions you can provide to address those concerns. Remember that everyone has a problem, and they will only pay if your solution solves their problem. Furthermore, identifying actual problems and developing effective solutions is key to making money from them.

Here are some ways to monetize problems:

- **Market Potential**: Assess demand. People can assess and validate identified problems by conducting idea extraction interviews to find problems that people are willing to pay to have them handled. This guarantees that efforts are focused on important issues with significant impact.
- **Consulting Firm**: Own and operate your own consulting firm. Provide problem-solving services to clients and earn money.
- **Product Development**: Create solutions to identified challenges. Entrepreneurs can establish successful businesses by testing assumptions and undertaking product discovery.

D. Opportunities

Making money from opportunities entails recognizing and capitalizing on favorable circumstances, trends, or situations. Remember that discovering opportunities takes a combination of research, creativity and adaptability. Please note that adequate preparation is very important when it comes to monetization.

When opportunity meets preparation, there comes success. Many people have missed valuable opportunities that may have changed their lives due to a lack of preparedness. Others have wealth now because they were ready when the opportunity presented itself. I know of a friend who purchased a vehicle at an affordable price because the owner was travelling outside the country and needed to sell the vehicle for money. He asked him how much he could afford, and that was all. He got it and could have spent five times as much for it. Prepare to take calculated risks and work hard to capitalize on the opportunities you discover.

Here are some ways to monetize opportunities:

- **Entrepreneurship**: Start a business that addresses a growing demand or fills a gap in the market.
- **Investing**: Invest in stocks, real estate, or other assets that have potential for growth.
- **Partnerships and Collaborations:** Partner with others to share resources, expertise and risk.
- **Trendspotting**: Identify emerging trends and create products or services that cater to them.
- **Event Planning**: Organize conferences, workshops, or events that bring people together and offer valuable experiences.

- **Selling Products or Services Online**: Utilize e-commerce platforms or social media to reach a wider audience.
- **Creating and Selling an Online Course**: Share expertise and teach others a valuable skill or knowledge.
- **Drop-shipping**: Sell products without holding any inventory by partnering with a supplier that ships products directly to customers.
- **Stock Photography**: Sell photos on stock image websites, such as **Shutter Stock** or **i-Stock**.
- **Participating in Gig economy**: Sign up with companies like Uber, Lyft, Door-Dash, or Postmates, and make money by delivering food or providing transportation.

E. Gifts and Talents

Making money from your God-given gifts and talents is not only possible but also rewarding. Identifying your gifts or talents and taking effective actions based on them is significant. Begin by listing your skills and determining how you may apply them to benefit others. With determination and creativity, you can transform your gifts and talents into a reliable source of revenue.

Some people have explicit talents, while others still have not discovered what they are truly capable of, but we all have some gifts and talents. God did not create you without giving you a gift or talent. It is your responsibility to carefully identify the gift or talent bestowed upon you for the benefit of the world.

Remember, turning your gifts and talents into income requires creativity, hard work, and a willingness to continuously develop and improve your skills.

Here are some ways to turn your gifts and talents into income:

- **Performing or entertaining**: Monetize your musical, artistic, or performance talents or gifts through gigs, concerts, or shows.

- **Selling handmade products**: Utilize platforms like Etsy or Redbubble to sell handmade products that showcase your artistic talents.

- **Licensing your work**: License your creative work, such as photos, music, or art, for use by others.

- **Creating a YouTube channel or Twitch stream**: Monetize your talents through ads, sponsorships and merchandise sales.

- **Creating an online membership or subscription-based service**: Offer exclusive content, resources, or support to members who pay a recurring fee.

- **Offering commissioned work**: Create custom pieces or services for clients who pay for your expertise.

F. Product & Services

Making money from products and services entails developing and providing value to clients in exchange for payment. Remember that making money from products and services requires knowing your target audience, advertising effectively, and providing value that meets or exceeds client expectations.

Here are some ways to monetize products and services:

- **Selling physical products**: Manufacture and sell tangible products through online marketplaces, retail stores, or direct sales.

- **Offering digital products**: Create and sell intangible products like eBooks, software, and online courses.

- **Providing services**: Offer expertise and skills through consulting, coaching, freelancing, or agency services.

- **Subscription-based models**: Offer recurring access to products or services for a monthly or annual fee.

- **Licensing and royalties**: License products or intellectual property and earn royalties from sales or usage.

- **Advertising and sponsorships**: Sell ad space or partner with brands for sponsored content and offer web services, such as website designing and development.

G. Dreams & Visions

Generating money from dreams and visions involves turning your spiritual revelations into reality through entrepreneurship, innovation and creativity. The Holy Scriptures tell us the account of Daniel the Jew and Joseph,

Jacob's son, and how these two people were nobody. Daniel was even thrown into the lion's den for disobeying the King's orders, while Joseph was imprisoned due to false accusations.

However, they were elevated to the position of prime minister after correctly interpreting the Kings' dreams. Please refer to **Genesis 41** and **Daniel 2** for more details of the stories. Joseph's interpretation and wise counsel save the people of Egypt from death due to the severe famine.

I heard the story of a successful popcorn business owner who was inspired by her dream to leave Europe for her country to start a popcorn business. The exact location and name of her business were revealed to her in the dream. She was initially adamant, but since the dream kept appearing, she eventually decided to return home and start the popcorn business. She expressed sorrow for spending so many years in Europe with little to show for it. However, she is now wealthy and has a large workforce working for her in various branches and sales locations. Please don't joke with things revealed to you in your dreams and visions, as they can help you discover your purpose on this earth.

Here are some ways to monetize your dreams and visions:

- **Start a business**: Turn your vision into a product or service that solves a problem or meets a need in the market.

- **Create a product or invention**: Develop a unique product or invention that embodies your dream or vision.
- **Write a book or create a course**: Share your knowledge and expertise through a book or online course.
- **License your idea**: Sell your idea or concept to a company or individual who can develop and market it.
- **Partner with others**: Collaborate with like-minded individuals or companies to bring your vision to life.
- **Develop a software or tool**: Create a software or tool that solves a problem or makes a process easier.
- **Create an online community or forum**: Build a community around your vision and monetize through advertising, sponsorships and affiliate marketing.
- **Offer consulting or coaching services**: Share your expertise and help others achieve their goals.
- **Create a video series or documentary**: Share your vision through a video series or documentary and monetize through ads or sponsorships.

H. Partnership/Networks/Groups/People

Generating money from partnerships and networks involves collaborating with others to create value and share revenue. Remember, generating money from partnerships and networks requires building strong relationships, setting clear agreements and delivering value to all parties involved. Generating money from people also involves offering value, services, or products that meet their needs, wants, or interests. Finally, generating money from people requires building trust, offering value and understanding their needs and interests.

Here are some ways to monetize partnerships, networks, groups and people:

- **Joint Ventures**: Partner with others to develop a product, service, or business, sharing profits and risks.
- **Affiliate Marketing**: Promote partners' products or services and earn a commission for each sale made through your unique referral link.
- **Strategic Partnerships**: Collaborate with complementary businesses to expand offerings and revenue streams.
- **Network Marketing**: Build a network of distributors or partners to sell products or services, earning commissions on sales.
- **Co-Marketing**: Partner with others to share marketing efforts and costs, expanding reach and revenue.
- **Licensing Agreements**: License products, services, or intellectual property to partners, earning royalties.
- **Franchising**: Offer a business model or brand for others to replicate, earning fees and royalties.

- **Supply Chain Partnerships**: Collaborate with suppliers to reduce costs, improve efficiency and increase profits.
- **Revenue Sharing**: Share revenue with partners who drive traffic, sales, or referrals.
- **API Partnerships**: Integrate with other companies' APIs to expand offerings and revenue streams.
- **Co-Creation**: Partner with others to develop new products, services, or experiences, sharing revenue and risks.
- **Distribution Partnerships**: Partner with others to expand distribution channels and reach new customers.
- **Technology Partnerships**: Collaborate with others to develop new technologies or integrate existing ones.
- **Marketing Alliances**: Partner with others to share marketing efforts and costs, expanding reach and revenue.
- **Business Development Partnerships**: Collaborate with others to identify new business opportunities and revenue streams.

I. Wisdom

Generating money from wisdom involves sharing your knowledge, insights and expertise with others, creating value that resonates with them and makes a positive impact. Wisdom can help you align your finances with your spiritual values and trust in God's abundance.

Here are some ways to monetize your wisdom:

- **Coaching or Consulting**: Offer guidance and advice to individuals or businesses, helping them navigate challenges and achieve goals.

- **Writing and Publishing**: Share your wisdom through books, eBooks, articles, or blogs, generating income through sales or advertising.

- **Speaking Engagements**: Share your wisdom through public speaking, keynote addresses, or workshops and earn fees or honorariums.

- **Online Courses or Tutorials**: Create digital content teaching others a skill or subject, selling through platforms like Udemy or Skillshare.

- **Mentorship Programs**: Offer one-on-one or group guidance, sharing your expertise and experience.

- **Podcasting or YouTube Channels**: Share your wisdom through audio or video content, generating income through sponsorships or ads.

- **Membership or Subscription-based Models**: Offer exclusive content, resources, or support for a recurring fee.

- **Workshops or Masterminds**: Host in-person or virtual events, sharing your wisdom and expertise with a group.

- **Licensing Your Expertise**: Allow others to use your intellectual property, such as copyrighted materials or trademarks, for a fee.

- **Creating and Selling an Online Community or Forum**: Build a platform for others to connect, share and learn from each other.
- **Offering Personalized Advice or Guidance**: Provide one-on-one support, helping others make informed decisions or navigate challenges.

J. God or Creator

God is the creator of the universe and owns everything therein. It is an undisputed fact that God blesses and favors those who obey and love Him. However, since God Almighty does not directly dispense money, He blesses people through the preceding mediums we have already discussed. We see many people crying for money when God has given them wisdom, ideas, gifts, talents, dreams and visions for them to monetize. However, because of a lack of understanding, they fail to take action and continue to complain and weep for money.

Others, too, lack an understanding of the times and seasons in which they find themselves and, as a result, refuse to utilize the downtime provided to prepare for the opportunity or breakthrough they seek. Instead, they focus on the present circumstances or problems, refusing to pay heed to the voice of God for the next step.

Here are some ways to generate income inspired by spiritual principles:

- **Tithing and Offerings**: Share a portion of your income with your place of worship or charitable causes, trusting in God's abundance.
- **Faith-based Entrepreneurship**: Start a business or create products/services that align with your values and beliefs, trusting God to guide and prosper your endeavors.
- **Spiritual Coaching or Counseling**: Offer guidance and support to others seeking spiritual growth and connection with God.
- **Creating Inspirational Content**: Write books, blogs, or create art that inspires and uplifts others, potentially generating income through sales or sponsorships.
- **Ministry Work**: Serve in various roles within your place of worship or community, potentially receiving compensation or support.
- **Prayer and Faith-based Services**: Offer prayer support, blessings, or other spiritual services to others, potentially receiving donations or offerings.
- **Charitable Work**: Engage in volunteer work or start a non-profit organization, potentially attracting funding or support from like-minded individuals.
- **Spiritual Retreats or Workshops**: Organize events or retreats focused on spiritual growth and connection, potentially generating income through registration fees or donations.

- **Inspirational Speaking**: Share your faith and message with others through public speaking engagements, potentially receiving compensation or support.
- **Gratitude and Trust**: Focus on cultivating a mindset of gratitude and trust in God's provision, potentially attracting abundance and prosperity into your life.

❖ *Budgeting*

After earning money, the next process of creating wealth is to develop a budget that aligns with your goals and helps you manage your income and expenses effectively. Track your spending, identify where to cut back, and prioritize saving and investing. Regularly review your budget and adjust as and when needed to stay on track. Cultivate habits of financial discipline. Practice delayed gratification by resisting impulsive purchases and focusing on long-term financial goals. Avoid unnecessary expenses and prioritize your spending based on your values and priorities. Develop a disciplined approach to saving and investing, even during challenging times.

Budgeting involves preparing anticipated income and expenses for a specific time frame, whether for personal use, family, or business. Budgeting is a great tool for planning and controlling scarce resources. It helps you understand where your money goes. By preparing and sticking to your budget, you increase your chances of following through on your plan and meeting your financial objectives. Budgets also discourage behaviors such as overspending, which can jeopardize your goals.

Consider What The Scripture Says Below:

Luke 14:28-30

28 For which of you, intending to build a tower, does not sit down first and count the cost, whether he has enough to finish it— 29 lest, after he has laid the foundation, and is not able to finish, all who see it begin to mock him, 30 saying, 'This man began to build and was not able to finish.'

The above Bible text underscores the significance of budgeting and planning for everyone striving for success in the world.

➢ ***Steps for Preparing a Budget***

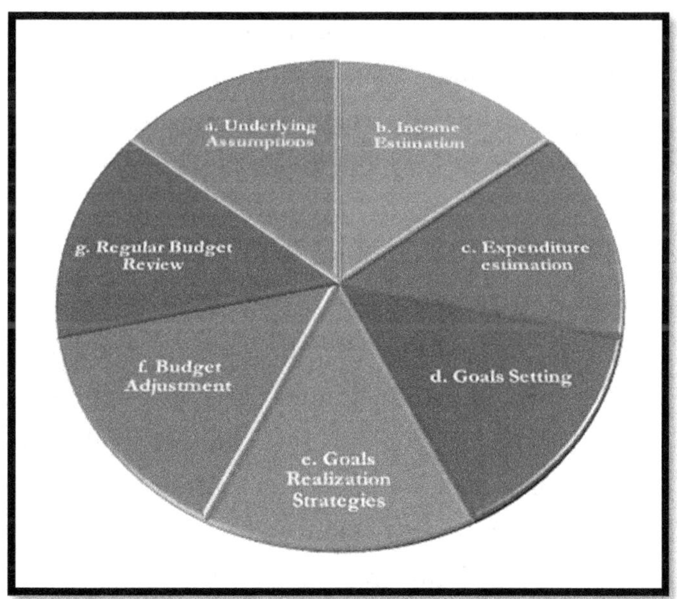

Figure 5.3

A. *Underlying Assumptions*

Assumptions are a very important aspect of budgeting. It is imperative to mention that your budget points towards the future, and therefore, you need to have the basis upon which you will make future projections about your income and expenditure. It will be extremely difficult to realize your goals without making proper assumptions, as any unanticipated factors can severely impact your budget.

Mostly, many individuals or entities make assumptions based on the factors mentioned below:

- **Actual Figures:** You can base your estimates on prior or current-year actual figures to project for the next period if all of the conditions that prompted the prior year or current performance are still in effect.

- **Inflation:** You should consider the rate of inflation because it might have a substantial impact on your projections. Higher inflation diminishes purchasing power and raises the cost of general goods and services. If inflation continues to rise, it will be difficult to meet your objectives without appropriate measures.

- **Fuel Price Hikes:** An increase in the price of gasoline at the pump has an impact on transportation, and as a result, the general prices of products and services are typically adjusted to reflect this increase. You need to ascertain the prices of fuel and factor them into your projections if you anticipate an increase.

- **Foreign Currency Exchange:** If you import some of your business's raw materials or products for manufacturing or sales, you will suffer greatly, especially if the foreign currency fluctuates. Try to understand the foreign currency situation at the time of projection and incorporate it if necessary.

- **Global Recession:** A recession is referred to as a general decrease in global economic activity. It is necessary to consider the current status of global economic activity. When things go wrong on a global scale, it has a significant influence on many countries, and individuals and businesses suffer as a result. Look at how the COVID-19 pandemic and the Russia-Ukraine war affected the world.

- **Industry Outlook:** If you want to have a workable budget, you should also consider the outlook of the industry to which you belong. Changes in your industry can also affect your business performance. Your budget assumptions must also reflect these industry changes.

- **National Economic Condition:** Lastly, your budget assumptions must also consider your national economic situation, such as changes in the tax laws, new legislations, etc.

B. Income Estimation

The next step in the budget preparation process after the budget assumptions is the projection of all your expected income. At this point, you are expected to determine your various streams of income and the total amount of income to be derived from each source. Some of your income can include revenue from your business, net salaries, gains on investments, allowances, overtime, income from rentals, etc.

C. Expenditure Estimation

After you have projected your income, the next step is to estimate how you will spend it. That is where your income will go. Before projecting your variable expenses, such as shopping and entertainment, make a list of your fixed expenses. These include utilities, housekeeping, groceries, school fees, housing charges, regular repairs and maintenance, and your monthly savings amount. Fixed expenses are monthly expenses that are regular, whereas variable expenses change from month to month. As previously discussed, you may use the **20%/80% rule**. You spend **20%** of your money on savings and investments, and the remaining **80%** on needs **(50%)** and wants **(30%)**.

D. Goal-Setting

It is important to understand that your goals are heavily dependent on your income, as you can only spend what you have. Make sure your short-term goals are specific, measurable, achievable, realistic and time-bound. Any unrealistic goal can discourage you from working harder and sticking to your budget because you might not be able to realize it. Your goals could be to purchase land or a vehicle, pay off a mortgage, or cover second-degree tuition costs.

E. Goals Realization Strategies

These are the strategies you are going to use to realize the goals that you have set for yourself. Here, try to juxtapose your estimated income with your expenditure. This will help you know whether you will be overspending your budget. You need to cut off extra fat (expenses) if necessary so that you can stick to your budget. **Focus more on your needs than your wants**. You may have to work hard to increase your customer base and sales or take a part-time job to boost your income.

F. Budget Adjustment

Any of the underlying budget assumptions listed earlier are subject to change. Flex your budget to reflect any significant changes that can severely affect your goals.

G. Regular Budget Review

You need to monitor your income and expenses by comparing them with your budget to see whether you are on course or not. Regular review of your figures is very crucial, as they will help you either stay with your current strategies or revise them when necessary.

I have provided a personal or family budget template below for your study.

PERSONAL / FAMILY BUDGET

INCOME	JAN	FEB	MAR	APR	MAY	JUN	JUL	AUG	SEP	OCT	NOV	DEC	TOTAL
Personal Monthly Business I	0.00	0.00	0.00	0.00	0.00	0.00	0.00	0.00	0.00	0.00	0.00	0.00	-
Monthly Net Income	0.00	0.00	0.00	0.00	0.00	0.00	0.00	0.00	0.00	0.00	0.00	0.00	-
Royalties	0.00	0.00	0.00	0.00	0.00	0.00	0.00	0.00	0.00	0.00	0.00	0.00	-
interest	0.00	0.00	0.00	0.00	0.00	0.00	0.00	0.00	0.00	0.00	0.00	0.00	-
dividends	0.00	0.00	0.00	0.00	0.00	0.00	0.00	0.00	0.00	0.00	0.00	0.00	-
Capital gains	0.00	0.00	0.00	0.00	0.00	0.00	0.00	0.00	0.00	0.00	0.00	0.00	-
Refunds or Reimbursements	0.00	0.00	0.00	0.00	0.00	0.00	0.00	0.00	0.00	0.00	0.00	0.00	-
Transfer From Savings	0.00	0.00	0.00	0.00	0.00	0.00	0.00	0.00	0.00	0.00	0.00	0.00	-
Gifts	0.00	0.00	0.00	0.00	0.00	0.00	0.00	0.00	0.00	0.00	0.00	0.00	-
Rent Income	0.00	0.00	0.00	0.00	0.00	0.00	0.00	0.00	0.00	0.00	0.00	0.00	-
Equipment Rental	0.00	0.00	0.00	0.00	0.00	0.00	0.00	0.00	0.00	0.00	0.00	0.00	-
Fees	0.00	0.00	0.00	0.00	0.00	0.00	0.00	0.00	0.00	0.00	0.00	0.00	-
Prizes & Awards	0.00	0.00	0.00	0.00	0.00	0.00	0.00	0.00	0.00	0.00	0.00	0.00	-
Tips	0.00	0.00	0.00	0.00	0.00	0.00	0.00	0.00	0.00	0.00	0.00	0.00	-
Patent/Copyright Income	0.00	0.00	0.00	0.00	0.00	0.00	0.00	0.00	0.00	0.00	0.00	0.00	-
Grants	0.00	0.00	0.00	0.00	0.00	0.00	0.00	0.00	0.00	0.00	0.00	0.00	-
Commissions	0.00	0.00	0.00	0.00	0.00	0.00	0.00	0.00	0.00	0.00	0.00	0.00	-
TOTAL INCOME	-	-	-	-	-	-	-	-	-	-	-	-	-
EXPENDITURE													
Transportation	0.00	0.00	0.00	0.00	0.00	0.00	0.00	0.00	0.00	0.00	0.00	0.00	-
Repairs and Maintenance	0.00	0.00	0.00	0.00	0.00	0.00	0.00	0.00	0.00	0.00	0.00	0.00	-
Medical Expenses	0.00	0.00	0.00	0.00	0.00	0.00	0.00	0.00	0.00	0.00	0.00	0.00	-
Gifts	0.00	0.00	0.00	0.00	0.00	0.00	0.00	0.00	0.00	0.00	0.00	0.00	-
Charitable Donations	0.00	0.00	0.00	0.00	0.00	0.00	0.00	0.00	0.00	0.00	0.00	0.00	-
Religious Donations	0.00	0.00	0.00	0.00	0.00	0.00	0.00	0.00	0.00	0.00	0.00	0.00	-
Groceries	0.00	0.00	0.00	0.00	0.00	0.00	0.00	0.00	0.00	0.00	0.00	0.00	-
Personal Supplies	0.00	0.00	0.00	0.00	0.00	0.00	0.00	0.00	0.00	0.00	0.00	0.00	-
Clothing	0.00	0.00	0.00	0.00	0.00	0.00	0.00	0.00	0.00	0.00	0.00	0.00	-
Cleaning	0.00	0.00	0.00	0.00	0.00	0.00	0.00	0.00	0.00	0.00	0.00	0.00	-
Education or Lessons	0.00	0.00	0.00	0.00	0.00	0.00	0.00	0.00	0.00	0.00	0.00	0.00	-
Dining or Eating Out	0.00	0.00	0.00	0.00	0.00	0.00	0.00	0.00	0.00	0.00	0.00	0.00	-
Salon & Barber	0.00	0.00	0.00	0.00	0.00	0.00	0.00	0.00	0.00	0.00	0.00	0.00	-
Pet Food	0.00	0.00	0.00	0.00	0.00	0.00	0.00	0.00	0.00	0.00	0.00	0.00	-
Newspaper	0.00	0.00	0.00	0.00	0.00	0.00	0.00	0.00	0.00	0.00	0.00	0.00	-
Magazines	0.00	0.00	0.00	0.00	0.00	0.00	0.00	0.00	0.00	0.00	0.00	0.00	-
Membership Dues	0.00	0.00	0.00	0.00	0.00	0.00	0.00	0.00	0.00	0.00	0.00	0.00	-
Bank Fees	0.00	0.00	0.00	0.00	0.00	0.00	0.00	0.00	0.00	0.00	0.00	0.00	-
Postage	0.00	0.00	0.00	0.00	0.00	0.00	0.00	0.00	0.00	0.00	0.00	0.00	-
Books	0.00	0.00	0.00	0.00	0.00	0.00	0.00	0.00	0.00	0.00	0.00	0.00	-
Games	0.00	0.00	0.00	0.00	0.00	0.00	0.00	0.00	0.00	0.00	0.00	0.00	-
Fun Stuff	0.00	0.00	0.00	0.00	0.00	0.00	0.00	0.00	0.00	0.00	0.00	0.00	-
Hobbies	0.00	0.00	0.00	0.00	0.00	0.00	0.00	0.00	0.00	0.00	0.00	0.00	-
Media	0.00	0.00	0.00	0.00	0.00	0.00	0.00	0.00	0.00	0.00	0.00	0.00	-
Outdoor Recreation	0.00	0.00	0.00	0.00	0.00	0.00	0.00	0.00	0.00	0.00	0.00	0.00	-
Sports	0.00	0.00	0.00	0.00	0.00	0.00	0.00	0.00	0.00	0.00	0.00	0.00	-
Toys & Gadgets	0.00	0.00	0.00	0.00	0.00	0.00	0.00	0.00	0.00	0.00	0.00	0.00	-
Vacation & Travel	0.00	0.00	0.00	0.00	0.00	0.00	0.00	0.00	0.00	0.00	0.00	0.00	-
Emergency Fund	0.00	0.00	0.00	0.00	0.00	0.00	0.00	0.00	0.00	0.00	0.00	0.00	-
Car Replacement	0.00	0.00	0.00	0.00	0.00	0.00	0.00	0.00	0.00	0.00	0.00	0.00	-
Retirement Fund	0.00	0.00	0.00	0.00	0.00	0.00	0.00	0.00	0.00	0.00	0.00	0.00	-
Investments	0.00	0.00	0.00	0.00	0.00	0.00	0.00	0.00	0.00	0.00	0.00	0.00	-
Education Fund	0.00	0.00	0.00	0.00	0.00	0.00	0.00	0.00	0.00	0.00	0.00	0.00	-
Student Loans	0.00	0.00	0.00	0.00	0.00	0.00	0.00	0.00	0.00	0.00	0.00	0.00	-
Credit Card Debt	0.00	0.00	0.00	0.00	0.00	0.00	0.00	0.00	0.00	0.00	0.00	0.00	-
Other Loans	0.00	0.00	0.00	0.00	0.00	0.00	0.00	0.00	0.00	0.00	0.00	0.00	-
Child Support	0.00	0.00	0.00	0.00	0.00	0.00	0.00	0.00	0.00	0.00	0.00	0.00	-
Federal Taxes	0.00	0.00	0.00	0.00	0.00	0.00	0.00	0.00	0.00	0.00	0.00	0.00	-
State or Local Taxes	0.00	0.00	0.00	0.00	0.00	0.00	0.00	0.00	0.00	0.00	0.00	0.00	-
Sewer or Trash	0.00	0.00	0.00	0.00	0.00	0.00	0.00	0.00	0.00	0.00	0.00	0.00	-
Project Expenses	0.00	0.00	0.00	0.00	0.00	0.00	0.00	0.00	0.00	0.00	0.00	0.00	-
Mortgage payment	0.00	0.00	0.00	0.00	0.00	0.00	0.00	0.00	0.00	0.00	0.00	0.00	-
Rent or accommodation	0.00	0.00	0.00	0.00	0.00	0.00	0.00	0.00	0.00	0.00	0.00	0.00	-
Home Insurance	0.00	0.00	0.00	0.00	0.00	0.00	0.00	0.00	0.00	0.00	0.00	0.00	-
Electricity	0.00	0.00	0.00	0.00	0.00	0.00	0.00	0.00	0.00	0.00	0.00	0.00	-
Gas	0.00	0.00	0.00	0.00	0.00	0.00	0.00	0.00	0.00	0.00	0.00	0.00	-
Water	0.00	0.00	0.00	0.00	0.00	0.00	0.00	0.00	0.00	0.00	0.00	0.00	-
Phone	0.00	0.00	0.00	0.00	0.00	0.00	0.00	0.00	0.00	0.00	0.00	0.00	-
Cable or Satellite	0.00	0.00	0.00	0.00	0.00	0.00	0.00	0.00	0.00	0.00	0.00	0.00	-
Internet	0.00	0.00	0.00	0.00	0.00	0.00	0.00	0.00	0.00	0.00	0.00	0.00	-
Furnishings & Appliances	0.00	0.00	0.00	0.00	0.00	0.00	0.00	0.00	0.00	0.00	0.00	0.00	-
Lawn	0.00	0.00	0.00	0.00	0.00	0.00	0.00	0.00	0.00	0.00	0.00	0.00	-
Supplies	0.00	0.00	0.00	0.00	0.00	0.00	0.00	0.00	0.00	0.00	0.00	0.00	-
Improvements	0.00	0.00	0.00	0.00	0.00	0.00	0.00	0.00	0.00	0.00	0.00	0.00	-
Other Expenses	0.00	0.00	0.00	0.00	0.00	0.00	0.00	0.00	0.00	0.00	0.00	0.00	-
TOTAL EXPENDITURE	-	-	-	-	-	-	-	-	-	-	-	-	-
OPERATING SURPLUS	0.00	0.00	0.00	0.00	0.00	0.00	0.00	0.00	0.00	0.00	0.00	0.00	-

Table 5.2

BUDGET ASSUMPTIONS:

1. VAT has been increased by 2.5% making it 15%. This will lead to increase in general prices of goods and services

2. Fuel Price Hikes Resulting in higher prices of Goods and Services

3. Inflation is at 54.2%. This will continue to affect the prices of Goods and Services

4. Depreciation of the local currency which affect cost of trading in transactions denominated in foreign currencies

5. Other running expenses are to increase averaging according to Market prices.

Figure 5.4

The above depicts what a simple budget looks like. As I previously stated, when it comes to budgeting, you are just trying to forecast your income and expenditure based on your underlying budget assumptions. Feel free to adopt the above budget template for your personal use.

Take note that not all of the income and expenditures indicated in the budget may apply to you. Please feel free to add any income and expenses that are not on the list and remove those that are not applicable when preparing your own budget.

➤ *Importance of Budgeting*
- **Controlling Spending Habits:** Without a budget, you can easily overspend and lose track of your costs. Budgeting allows you to comprehend the impact of seemingly minor expenses and gain control over your spending.

- **Sticking to Financial Goals:** A budget ensures that funds are allocated toward your objectives (such as saving, investing, or debt repayment). It helps you remain focused and accountable.
- **Financial Satisfaction:** Knowing where your money goes gives you peace of mind. You will be more pleased and less anxious about money.
- **Financial Burden Reduction:** A budget eliminates surprises and allows you to plan for regular expenses, decreasing financial stress.
- **Debt Reduction:** By properly spending your funds, you can pay off debt faster and prevent accruing interests.
- **Planning:** Having a budget makes it easier to manage your savings and investments, pay your expenses and organize your finances.
- **Emergency Planning:** One useful technique for increasing the size of your emergency savings is a budget. Making a budget guarantees that you save money for unforeseen costs.
- **Increased Savings:** Whether for long-term or short-term objectives, a budget helps you save regularly.
- **Future Financial Security:** You can reach your financial objectives more quickly and have a better future with proper budgeting.

❖ *Savings*

After you have set your goals, earned money, and created a budget, the next step is to save a percentage of your earnings. Saving involves setting aside income for future use, often through bank deposits, securities purchases, or increased cash holdings.

Why does saving money seem like a daunting task? Is it because of the immediate gratification that spending offers, or is it a lack of understanding about the importance of savings? Let's delve into the world of savings and give you some effective strategies to help you save more effectively.

It is also important to debunk the myth that savings are only for the wealthy. The truth is that everyone can save, irrespective of the size of their income. It all boils down to a simple principle, which is to spend less than you earn.

It is not rocket science, but it does require discipline and a clear understanding of your financial goals.

Many people believe that the **20/80 savings rule** emanated from the counsel Joseph gave to King Pharaoh in **Genesis 41:33-36** and Genesis **47:23-24** when there was severe famine in the land of Egypt. **Genesis 41:33-36** read as follows:

33 "And now let Pharaoh look for a discerning and wise man and put him in charge of the land of Egypt.

34 Let Pharaoh appoint commissioners over the land to take a fifth of the harvest of Egypt during the seven years of abundance.

35 They should collect all the food of these good years that are coming and store up the grain under the authority of Pharaoh, to be kept in the cities for food.

36 This food should be held in reserve for the country, to be used during the seven years of famine that will come upon Egypt, so that the country may not be ruined by the famine."

Genesis 47: 23-24 adds that:

23 Joseph said to the people, "Now that I have bought you and your land today for Pharaoh, here is seed for you so you can plant the ground.

*24 But when the crop comes in, give a fifth of it to Pharaoh. The other four-fifths you may **keep as seed for** the fields and as food for yourselves and your households and your children."*

The 20/80 rule of savings is an easy way to budget. It proposes that you save **20%** of your take-home money or income and spend the remaining **80%** on expenses. The first **20%** of your income should be automatically allocated to savings, investments, or debt repayment, beginning with an emergency fund that covers three to six months of your expenses. The guideline emphasizes setting aside adequate money in case of financial distress.

You pay yourself first by setting aside money for your long-term financial goals. Ideally, the majority of the money should go to retirement investments, as financial advisors typically recommend saving at least **15 to 20%** of your earnings aside for retirement.

The remaining **80%** is allocated to **needs (50%)** and **wants (30%)**, such as food, rent and entertainment. However, you have the liberty to spend the remaining money as you desire. The crucial component of this rule is that you should devote at least **20%** of your income to your long-term financial goals. Make savings a priority and set aside a portion of your income regularly, even if it is a tiny amount.

Consider the following strategies to set aside additional money for savings:

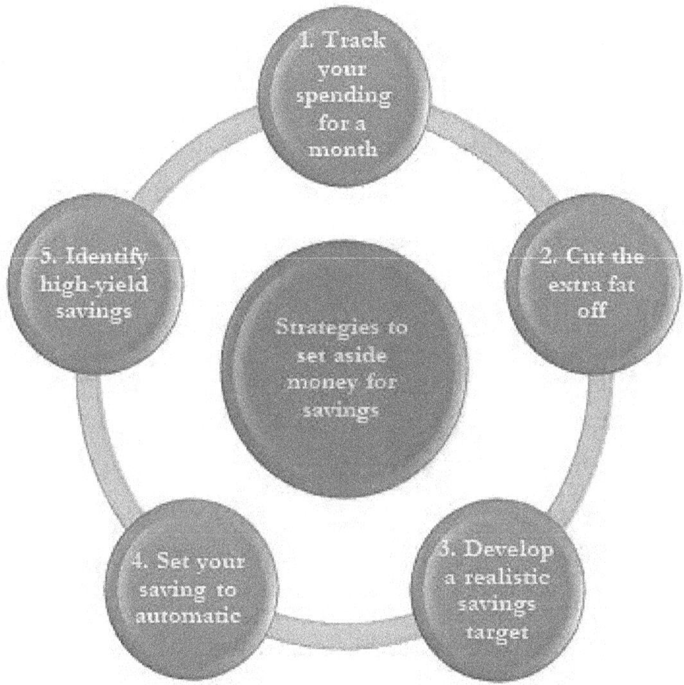

Figure 5.5

- **Track Your Spending for a Month**: You can use a budgeting tool or spreadsheet to assist you with this, and if you can't, a small, pocket-sized notebook would also suffice. Record everything you spend, even if it is a small amount; many people are startled to find where all their money goes.

- **Cut the Extra Fat off**: It simply means being more mindful about the things you spend your money on. Consider this: do you really need that daily takeaway coffee or food, or could you make it at home for a fraction of the cost? Small changes can make a big difference over time. Every little bit adds up and can boost your savings significantly.

  Divide your expenses between **needs and wants**. Food, housing, and clothing are **certainly needs**. Include health insurance costs, auto insurance if you own a car, and life insurance if others rely on your income. Many other expenses will be **merely wants**.

- **Develop a Realistic Savings Target**: If your goals are too lofty, you may become discouraged and give up. However, if they are achievable, you will be motivated to keep going and watch your savings grow.

  Once you have an idea of how much money you can set aside periodically, make an effort to keep to it. This does not imply that you must always live cheaply. If you are hitting your savings targets, feel free to treat yourself well once in a while. You will feel better and more inspired to stay on course.

- **Set Your Savings to Automatic**: One of the easiest ways to save is to set up automatic transfers from your employer or bank account to your savings account. In this manner, you are not tempted to spend the money, and it grows without your knowledge. So long as you refrain from making withdrawals, the accumulated money will earn compound interest. The beauty of compound interest is that your funds will increase faster than you might expect.

Select a specific amount from your earnings periodically and have it sent to your savings or investing account. Similarly, you can save for retirement by having contributions regularly deducted from your earnings and deposited into your account with pension trustees.

- **Identify High-Yield Savings:** Maximize the return on your savings by looking for savings accounts with the highest interest rates and lowest fees. A **high-yield savings account (HYSA)** pays a higher interest rate than a conventional savings account. **Certificates of deposit (CDs)** or **fixed deposits** might be an excellent savings choice if you can afford to keep the money for several months or years.

Savings accounts can accrue either simple or compound interest, depending on the type of bank and the agreement. To be directed and make an informed decision, you must first understand the type of interest being given.

Let's look at the illustrations below to better understand simple and compound interest on savings.

For example, for a **$1,000** borrowed amount with a **simple interest rate** of **5.00%** to be paid **annually for five years** and left untouched for the deposit period, **the simple interest calculation is:**

$1,000.00 x .05 x 5 = $250.00

Here is the interest broken out by year:

Year 1: $1,000.00 x .05 = $50.00 interest

Year 2: $1,000.00 x .05 = $50.00 interest

Year 3: $1,000.00 x .05 = $50.00 interest

Year 4: $1,000.00 x .05 = $50.00 interest

Year 5: $1,000.00 x .05 = $50.00 interest

Total interest over five years = $250.00

In a savings scenario, simple interest will pay the depositor less in total interest than compound interest because the interest payment is calculated on only the original principal.

A deposit account with compound interest would receive more in total interest than one with simple interest over the same length of time. Compound interest is compounded daily, monthly, or annually, and the frequency is stated in the account agreement.

For example, for a **$1,000** savings account balance with a **compound interest rate** of **5.00%** to be paid **annually for five years** and left untouched for the deposit period, the increase in principal and the new interest for each year is:

Year 1: $1,000.00 x .05 = $50.00 interest

Year 2: $1,050.00 x .05 = $52.50 interest

Year 3: $1,102.50 x .05 = $55.125 Interest

Year 4: $1,157.625 x .05 = $57.881 interest

Year 5: $1,215.506 x .05 = $60.775 interest

Total interest over five years = $276.281

➢ *Importance of Savings*

- **Financial Freedom:** Savings offer financial freedom, allowing individuals to make choices based on their desires, free from financial constraints.
- **Financial Stress:** Saving money can help relieve financial stress by minimizing anxiety about unforeseen expenses. It gives you a sense of security, which allows you to sleep better, pay your recurring bills on time, and feel relieved about income loss or unforeseen expenses.
- **Emergency Fund:** Savings help build an emergency fund, which is crucial for covering unanticipated expenses such as medical bills, natural occurrences, house maintenance, and family emergencies. They provide peace of mind and ensure that you do not struggle to cover living costs.
- **Savings help in meeting your investment needs**.
- **Retirement:** It helps in planning for a better retirement because it can appreciate in value and earn interest, compounding for faster growth.
- **Legacy for Future Generations:** Prioritizing saving involves implementing a financial strategy that improves wealth, fosters positive habits, and improves investment cash reserves, thereby fostering a legacy for future generations.
- **Opportunities:** Savings enable individuals to seize opportunities such as investing, starting a new business, or pursuing further education when they arise.

- **Compound Interest:** Savings help you take advantage of compound interest. With compound interest, the interest earned on your savings will also earn interest if you continue to save for a long time. This is a wonderful strategy to increase your income.
- **Debt Avoidance:** Regular savings can help prevent high-interest debt by allowing you to use your own funds for necessary expenses instead of borrowing.
- **Save for Recurring Expenses:** Extra savings can prevent emergency fund dips, as you can always rely on savings for any recurring bill payment when it becomes necessary.

➢ *Documents Required to Open a Savings Account with a Bank*

- **National Identification:** You must produce a government-issued ID, such as a driver's license or passport, which is a legal document identifying you as a citizen.
- **Social Security (Pension) Number:** Some banks accept your Taxpayer Identification Number (TIN) as an alternative to a Social Security number.
- **Proof of Residential Address:** A utility bill, credit card statement, or other verifiable document containing your name and address might serve as proof of residence.

- **Contact Information:** When you open a savings account, the bank will seek your contact information as well as that of your next of kin.
- **Bank Account Information:** You will be required to meet initial deposit requirements, so have your account and routing details ready as soon as your savings account is opened.
- **Passport-size Pictures:** The bank will usually demand two passport-size pictures for the account opening.

➤ *Advantages of Saving Money at Home*

- **Easy Access:** Saving money at home offers easy access to your money, eliminating stress and queuing.
- **No Bank Charges:** Saving money at home offers the advantage of not incurring bank charges on your savings.
- **Satisfaction:** Saving money at home provides satisfaction as you have a constant balance and can easily access it for spending without any documentation.

➤ *Disadvantages of Saving Money at Home*

- **Missed Investment Opportunities:** Saving money at home can lead to missed investment opportunities from banks and corporations, potentially increasing your net worth.

- **Risk of Loss:** Saving money at home comes with the disadvantage of the risk of losing it due to misplacement, theft or robbery.
- **Inflation Erosion:** Over time, inflation can decrease the purchasing power of your saved cash, making it a disadvantage to save money at home.
- **Damage:** Home-stored money may be improperly handled or stored in an unsafe location, leading to potential damage.
- **Lack of Insurance:** Saving money at home may not have insurance coverage for unexpected events, which can severely impact your financial stability.
- **No Interest:** Inflation can lead to a reduction in the value of money saved in a house, as it does not earn interest.
- **Change in Currency:** Another disadvantage of saving money at home is that you may not be able to use it if the government changes the currency, and you are unable to exchange your saved money for new currencies.

In summary, saving money doesn't have to be a chore. It is about spending less than you earn and tracking your expenses, automating your savings, cutting off the extra fat, identifying high-yield savings opportunities and setting realistic saving targets. With these strategies in mind, you will be well on your way to building a healthy savings account. Remember, it is not about how much you earn but how much you save that truly matters. So, start today and watch your savings grow.

❖ *Investment*

After saving money, the next process is investing the amount saved so that it will grow. Remember that interest rates on traditional savings accounts are comparatively low, and your money may lose purchasing power over time due to inflation.

Diversification is one of the most crucial investment principles for individual investors to understand. Simply put, your goal should be to distribute your funds among multiple investment portfolios. This is because investment performance varies over time. Bonds, for example, may provide excellent returns if the stock market is in decline.

Mutual funds offer some inherent diversification because they invest in a variety of securities. You will also gain more diversification if you invest in multiple stock and bond funds rather than in just one of them.

As a general rule, the younger you are, the more risk you can tolerate because you will have more years to recover from any losses. Invest your money prudently to create long-term wealth. Depending on your risk tolerance and financial goals, consider several investment options such as stocks, bonds, real estate and mutual funds.

Investments differ in terms of risk and potential return. Generally speaking, the safer they are, the smaller their prospective return, and vice versa. If you are unfamiliar with the various types of investments, it is a good idea to spend some time reading about them in **chapter four** of this book. While there are a variety of unusual investments, the majority of investors will prefer to begin with the basics: Treasury bills, stocks, bonds, mutual funds, etc.

Factors to consider before selecting an investment product:

Choosing the right investment for wealth creation might be difficult, but before selecting an investment product or option, you must carefully consider the following factors:

- **Investment Goals:** First of all, determine the reason why you want to invest. This will help you know whether your investment goal is short-term or long-term. Short-term goals require that you invest in securities that have a shorter maturity period, while long-term goals require investments with a longer maturity period.

  Examples of short-term investments are money market securities, which include **treasury bills, fixed deposits, repurchase agreements and commercial paper**.

  Long-term investments are capital market securities, which include **shares, bonds, mutual funds and derivatives.**

- **Risk:** Assess the risks involved in the investment option you have selected and analyze if they align with your investment goals. **Some of the risks to be**

considered are default risk, liquidity risk, and **market or economic risk.**

Some investors might not have as much liquidity as others, which makes buying or selling difficult. It is important to comprehend these limitations because they might lock in investments for certain periods of time.

- **Time Horizon:** It is important for you to consider the maturity period for the investment option that you intend to choose. The longer the maturity period, the higher the returns or gains. A shorter investment period usually offers lower returns or gains on your investment.

- **Returns:** Consider the returns or gains that will be accrued from investing in that particular security that you have selected for investment.

- **Fees:** Assess the charges associated with each investment option to guarantee the optimal return on your investment.

- **Tax Implication:** The majority of countries charge taxes on income or gains from investments. We refer to this tax as the **capital gains tax.** The tax rate varies from nation to nation and is subject to change whenever your government deems fit. When making an investment decision, it would be wise to inquire with tax specialists or investment advisors about the **capital gain tax rate.**

➢ *Reasons for Investing*
- To help grow your money.
- To earn a regular income.
- To meet financial goals.
- To protect your money from losing purchasing power.
- To keep your money safe.
- To maintain future financial stability.
- To meet unanticipated needs.
- To reduce financial dependence.
- To gain from capital appreciation.

➢ *Reasons Why People Do Not Invest*
- Saving money in a low-interest savings account.
- Waiting to have a higher salary before they invest.
- Trying to time the market.
- Perceiving investing as too risky.
- Feeling intimidated by the investment process.
- Thinking they have very little money to invest.
- Fear of losing money.
- The thought of having more time to save.
- Lack of financial education.

❖ *Protection of Assets*

You have worked hard to earn money and increase your wealth. The worst that can happen to you is losing everything due to a sudden tragedy or unforeseen event. It is very important to put measures in place as early as possible to safeguard all your hard-earned assets or resources.

Let's look at some of the asset protection measures below:

- **Insurance:** It is essential for developing money since it protects you from possible risks. Home insurance will replace your home and valuables if they are destroyed by fire, auto insurance will provide coverage for your property, liability and medical if you are involved in a car accident, and life insurance will give a death benefit to your beneficiaries if you die unexpectedly.

  Permanent disability insurance is another form of policy that will replace your income if you become wounded, ill, or otherwise incapacitated and are unable to work. Even young and healthy people should consider insurance products as they tend to become more expensive as you age. That means that even if you are twenty years old and unmarried, purchasing life insurance may be considerably cheaper than if you are 15 years older and have a family and a mortgage.

- **Due Diligence:** This is another method for safeguarding your hard-earned money. Due diligence is the process of conducting an inquiry or using reasonable care before entering into a contract or agreement with another party or before acting with a given degree of care.

You should constantly conduct extensive research and analysis on any new business or investment you wish to make. By doing this, you can avoid possible fraud and scams.

- **Investment Expert's Assistance:** You can also protect your wealth from possible threats by relying on the advice of investment or financial experts. You should always have reliable information, and these experts can easily assist you with the needed information and accurate analysis before making your final decision.

- **Prenuptial and Postnuptial Agreements:** These are contracts signed by married couples that specify terms of separation prior to and after marriage and guarantee the couple's decision to stay together.

Prenuptial and postnuptial agreements aim to achieve common marital objectives, including asset and debt sharing, financial rights delegation, testamentary disposition in the Last Will and Testament, and maintenance duration determination. Arbitration or mediation can be used to settle disputes among the couples.

It is imperative to mention that almost all the states in the United States of America accept prenuptial agreements, while only some of the states do accept postnuptial agreements.

- **Titling:** The titling of a home can significantly impact its protection against creditors. If both spouses own the home as tenants, they both own an indivisible interest, which can protect home equity in cases where state law does not offer a sufficient exemption. This option is only available in some states and applies to personal residences.

- **Limited Liability Companies (LLCs):** Limited liability companies (LLCs) operate according to the concept of a separate legal entity. This implies that you and your company are distinct entities. You and your company may sue and be sued individually.

If you are a business owner and are not a party to transactions or circumstances that give rise to a lawsuit, your personal assets are shielded from legal action.

❖ *Debt Management*

The next process of wealth creation is the use and management of debt. Many wealthy individuals have used debt to positively expand their businesses and fund capital-intensive projects and investments. Though having access to debt might provide you with sufficient relief, it is imperative to mention that the borrowed funds must be used for their intended purposes. This will help you pay off the principal and the interest when they become due.

It is crucial to manage your debt prudently, as taking on too much debt may inhibit your progress toward your wealth-creation goals. It is highly recommended for you to always **be outside debt** and **not inside debt."** This simply means that you should not borrow more than you have.

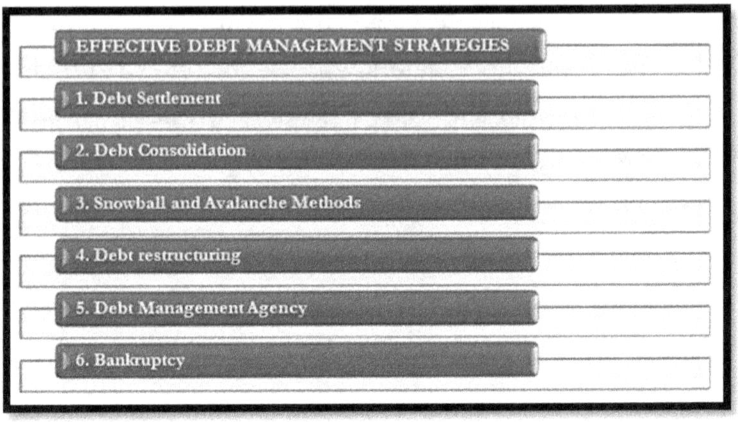

Figure 5.6

- **Debt Settlement**: This is a debt management strategy in which you negotiate with your creditors to accept a smaller payment than the full amount owed, thereby decreasing the total debt. This option can help you if you have large amounts of unsecured debt, but it may have a negative impact on your credit ratings and should be carefully examined.

- **Debt Consolidation**: This entails merging multiple debts into a single loan with better terms, such as reduced interest rates or longer repayment periods. This debt management strategy makes repayment easier and can help you save money on interest payments over time.

- **Snowball and Avalanche Methods**: The snowball and avalanche strategies are two prominent debt management strategies for paying off multiple debts. The snowball strategy prioritizes paying off debts with the smallest balances first, while the avalanche strategy focuses on debts with the highest interest rates. Both strategies can be useful in debt management, and the choice is based on personal preferences and financial circumstances.

- **Debt Restructuring**: It is a strategy adopted by organizations, individuals and even countries to avoid defaulting on existing debts. It entails negotiating with your creditors to lower the interest rate, prolong the payback period, or reduce the loan balance. It can help you manage your debt by allowing you to make smaller monthly payments and pay interest at a lower rate. For firms, debt restructuring might include a debt-for-equity swap, in which creditors agree to cancel a portion or all of the outstanding debt in return for equity in the business. Also, a company looking to restructure its debt may arrange with its bondholders to **"take a haircut,"** which means that a portion of the outstanding interest payments will be written off or a portion of the principal will not be repaid.

  Debt restructuring is a less expensive alternative to bankruptcy for debtors in financial distress, and it can be beneficial to both you and your lender.

- **Debt Management Agency**: Under this debt management strategy, you do not need to bargain directly with your lender. Instead, you may be able to seek the assistance of a debt management firm. These organizations often work with unsecured debt, such as credit card balances, and can negotiate lower interest rates, monthly payments, reduced fees and other terms with your creditors.

- **Bankruptcy**: Filing for bankruptcy is never a good idea, but if you have no other options, such as debt restructuring, it may be your final remedy. Bankruptcy can allow you to enter into a reformed repayment plan with your creditors or eliminate your debt entirely after liquidating part of your assets, giving you a fresh start. However, a bankruptcy filing can remain on your credit reports for up to a number of years, making it difficult to obtain credit for some time, so think carefully and speak with a financial advisor and bankruptcy expert before proceeding.

❖ *Continuous Financial Education*

This is one of the important processes of creating wealth. Knowledge is an effective tool for increasing wealth. Commit to continuous learning and self-improvement in personal finance and wealth creation. Stay up-to-date on financial trends, investment strategies and market developments. Read books, listen to financial audios and videos, follow credible financial experts and participate in workshops or seminars. The more knowledge you gain, the better equipped you are to make sound financial decisions.

❖   ***Strong Supportive Network***

Surround yourself with like-minded individuals who share your financial objectives and values. Engage in personal finance discussions, ask for help and share your experiences. A helpful network can offer encouragement, accountability and useful insights into your wealth-creation efforts.

❖   ***Commitment to the Long Term Goals***

Building wealth is a long-term process. Maintain your financial goals even when the market is volatile or you face personal issues. Avoid chasing short-term gains and instead focus on the broader picture. Maintain patience, discipline and continuous progress toward your financial goals.

Chapter 6|
Elements of Balanced Wealth

Wealth creation is a multi-dimensional journey requiring patience, effort, time and commitment. The wealth creation journey is not solely about amassing financial resources. It emphasizes holistic well-being, fostering healthy relationships and following passions that provide joy and fulfillment. By balancing financial prosperity and personal happiness, you can achieve a genuine sense of richness and live an abundant life.

To achieve financial independence and abundance, it is important to maintain balance in all areas of life. We should not desire fortune at the expense of our family and close friends. We must ensure that we do not disregard the most important aspects of our lives in our quest for wealth.

It will be unsatisfying to have deteriorated health, broken homes, and long-standing friendships destroyed while gaining a lot of wealth. We must not abandon our dreams just because we want to be wealthy. We may realize our objectives, manage many enterprises, have a beautiful family, and still be wealthy.

Many successful entrepreneurs assess their wealth using traditional means, such as money. There is enough money to support a desired lifestyle, provide for family members, and save for a happy retirement. There are even opportunities to experience some of life's true pleasures.

Certainly! When it comes to wealth, it is important to understand that it goes beyond only financial abundance. True wealth entails a holistic approach that goes beyond money.

Let's explore the six elements of balanced wealth:

A. Time

It is a valuable asset that helps to develop riches.

Figure 6.1

The most crucial question is: "What do you do with your time?" Many individuals nowadays crave comfort and prosperity, yet they waste their precious time on things that do not benefit them. Remember that time ticks away every day, and each day that passes is removed from the number of days you have left on this planet. Time wasted cannot be regained.

Time is of great essence, and you must spend it wisely. As the day approaches, you will be unable to perform active work. Also, if you refuse to do the work you are expected to do when you are young or strong, you will be obliged to work when you should be retiring and resting.

One thing I have noticed about the wealthy is that they do not enjoy wasting time because they recognize its importance. As Charles Darwin once remarked, "A man who wastes one hour of time has not discovered the value of life." You will rarely see the wealthy conversing with others, spending all day on social media chatting with them, or engaging in pointless talks that will not benefit them.

The wealthy love to read books, listen to news, and attend seminars and conferences to stay informed about new changes and developments in various fields of business and the global economy. These conferences expose them to new business opportunities and connections. They can also prepare ahead of time before the new changes take effect to minimize any impact on their lives and businesses.

On the other hand, the poor or average person does not recognize the value of time and how it can affect their wealth. I always pity people who spend all their time watching comedies and videos on social media that will not enrich their lives in any way. Some people do not even know that by spending their precious time watching videos on social media, they are helping content creators make more money while they remain poor.

Bill Gates, the founder of Microsoft, said, "If you are born poor, it's not your mistake, but if you die poor, it's your mistake." In reality, you have no control over which family you are born into. You can be born into a royal family and never work in your life, or you can be born poor. In any case, it will never prevent a truly motivated individual from realizing their ambition for success. However, if you die poor, it may be your fault because you may lack the determination to develop your wealth while having little or nothing.

You have to understand that no condition is permanent, and there is time for everything. As a result, you need to manage and apportion your time well for yourself, work, business, friends and family. Balancing work, leisure and personal time contributes significantly to overall well-being.

> ➢ *Important Facts about Time*
- **Time Is Life:** You will live longer and accomplish more of your goals if you have more time left on this planet. You don't, however, get to choose how long you should spend here on Earth. Use your time wisely as a result.
- **Time Is Money:** The only reason you get paid at work or for doing something is because time is seen as a valuable asset that should ideally translate into something of value. So remember that the more you waste your time, the more you deny yourself money, and the poorer you will become.
- **Time Cannot Be Borrowed:** Time is something you cannot borrow and add to yours. No matter how much people love you, they do not have the power

to deduct time from theirs and give it to you for survival.

- **Time Wasted Cannot Be Recovered:** The present is all the time you have. It is not possible to go back in time, make amends for your mistakes or regrets, and then return to the present. You cannot wish to be a child or to have another birth. You might not have these opportunities again if you choose not to take advantage of them now.

- **Time Cannot Be Bribed:** I have never seen, heard of, or read about someone who attempted to bribe time for them to have more life. Do you even know where the time is located?

- **Time Waits for No One:** Time has an owner who has set it to move forward at a certain pace. It cannot be made to stop moving, slow down, or move forward by force. Although you can pause your personal time or clock, the general time will not cease. You can ask employees how much they typically wish for time to pass more quickly in January, but they won't.

  Many students who were poorly prepared for their tests wished the exam period had never come. Unfortunately, their exam time moved faster and closer than they anticipated.

- **Time Is 24 Hours a Day for Everyone:** Everybody has 24 hours within the day. You decide what to do with yours.

- **Time Cannot Move Backwards:** Time does not roll backwards. Nobody can pray or do something for time to go back. I haven't heard or read about it.
- **Time Is Not Discriminatory:** Time is fair to everybody since we all have the same time within the day. Time is not controlled by human beings, who can decide to give some people more than others.
- **Time Moves Forward, yet Immortal:** Time is the only thing that moves forward and is not subject to death, unlike people whose lives on Earth are getting shorter by the day. Everyone came to meet time, and time will undoubtedly continue even after we all age and pass away.
- **Time Is Priceless:** Nobody can buy time with wealth or anything else. When it is your time to die, you will die, and nobody can do anything about it.
- **Time Cannot Be Timed:** It is interesting to note that time cannot be affected by time. There is time for everything except time itself.
- **Time Has Owner (God):** Everything in this universe, including time, was created by one person, who is God the Creator.
- **Time is a Factor for Success:** It is crucial to remember that how you use your time affects your success. Respect for time is a valuable asset that makes people far more successful than those who lack it. Time can be a factor in losing an opportunity.

- **Time Is Everything You Have**: Finally, you can do more if you have more time, and you can do less if you have less time. Similarly, you can live longer if you have more time, and you can die early if you have a short time.

> *Enemies of Time*

- **Procrastination:** The habit of delaying or postponing tasks that require urgent attention. This is one of the biggest enemies of people's time.
- **Laziness:** The tendency to avoid work leads to inefficiency. Laziness can limit opportunities and success. If you are too lazy to work or complete your tasks, you will delay or waste your time and have to utilize time that could have been spent doing something else to complete duties that you did not complete.
- **Idleness:** The state of being inactive or unproductive. You are essentially doing nothing, which might cause time to slip and hinder you from completing your goals or deadlines.
- **Repetition:** Doing the same work over and over again can delay your time.
- **Lack of Clear Objectives:** How can you begin a journey if you don't know your destination? You will waste your time if you don't know exactly what you are to do.
- **Lack of Planning and Organization:** If you fail to plan, you plan to fail. Improper or lack of planning

and organization can lead to avoidable mistakes, which will demand more of your time for correction.

You should stay away from distractions such as unexpected visits and social media (Facebook, Twitter, YouTube, Snapchat, Instagram, WhatsApp etc.).

People will use you for entertainment and stress relief if you don't let them know your schedule. They will frequently come to your house for gossip and unnecessary discussions.

One of the major enemies of people's time today is social media. If you are not disciplined, you will become addicted to it and will not do anything meaningful for yourself. It will control you, and you will help content creators make more money for themselves while you remain poor.

- **Television, Radio, Phone Calls:** Television and phones have become mini-gods in the lives of many people. The first thing they remember when they wake up is their phones, while others spend all day watching telenovelas.
- **Lack of Rest or Sleep:** If you lack adequate rest or sleep, it makes you unproductive. You will delay or waste your time because you will lose concentration and make mistakes, which will take much of your time to correct.
- **Lack of Courage to Say No:** If you are unable to say no to others when necessary, they will increase your

workload while living their own lives. You may take longer to complete your daily tasks or miss your deadline.

- **Lack of Knowledge and or Data:** I wonder what you can do without knowledge or the necessary data to work with.

- **Lack of Communications and Services (internet, electricity, etc.):** If there is no clear communication, you may do something and subsequently realize you did it incorrectly. Additionally, a lack of internet or energy can cause delays in your tasks.

- **Lack of Delegation (Doing too much at the same time):** If you do not learn how to delegate some of your work to subordinates, you will be overburdened and behind schedule.

Now take your time to study and understand the effective strategies for managing your time as outlined below:

- EFFECTIVE TIME MANAGEMENT STRATEGIES
- Know yourself
- Morning Devotion
- Plan your day with a to-do list
- Prepare an organized priority list
- Batch your time by grouping similar tasks together
- Divide larger projects or works into smaller tasks
- Focus on one thing at a time
- Block time off on your calendar
- Limit distractions
- Summarize and review your day

Figure 6.2

✓ *Know Yourself*

Nobody knows you better than yourself. Are you the type of person who values time and prefers to spend it on productive activities? If you don't value your own time, how can you expect others to do so? People will find something for you to do if they notice you being idle and doing needless things.

Start by doing a time audit to determine where you spend your time. Determine which areas generate more income, improvement, or benefit and which areas bring nothing to the table. You will realize that you need to devote more of your time to the most important aspects of your life.

Also, you have to be in control of your time and learn to say no to people when necessary so that you don't end up postponing your tasks for other people's work. You have to do a **SWOT analysis** to determine your strengths, weaknesses, opportunities and threats. This will help you know what works best for you and the strategies you need to put in place to manage your time. Some people are more productive at work or when studying in the morning; some work and learn well at night, while others prefer daytime.

✓ *Morning Devotion*

The first thing you need to do before beginning your day is to have your morning devotion. You can't tell exactly when you fell asleep, and being among the living is a treasure. Some people fall asleep and never regain consciousness. Others awaken from their sleep but are not the same as they were before. Someone may have protected you throughout the night, and the least you can do is express gratitude for their protection and love. You have to put the day in God's hands since you have no idea what it will bring.

✓ *Plan Your Day with a To-Do List*

Yogi Berra once said, **"If you don't know where you are going, you'll end up someplace else."** This means it is important to have direction, and planning your day with a to-do list will help you achieve your objectives for the day by not wasting time on unnecessary or less important things.

You must have your basic stationery, such as an address book, pen, calculator, calendar, and watch, to be effective. Thankfully, you can also make use of your digital tools, such as phones, iPads and laptops, for this purpose. List all the things that need to be done within the day.

✓ *Prepare an Organized Priority List*

At this stage, you can use what we call the scale of preferences. This scale allows you to prioritize tasks based on their importance, with critical tasks at the top and less satisfying ones at the bottom.

✓ *Batch Your Time by Grouping Similar Tasks Together*

This is where you try to group similar tasks that need to be done into groups. This will make you efficient by not switching tasks, and you can quickly knock them out. You will then focus the rest of the time on the other tasks listed, and by the time you realize it, you are done for the day. This time management strategy can be applied regardless of the specific job or industry.

✓ ***Divide Larger Projects or Works into Smaller Tasks***
Work overload often leads to poor time management, especially on large tasks or projects. Breaking projects into smaller, manageable tasks can help overcome this feeling, making it easier for you to start and progress, ultimately improving overall time management.

Delegating tasks to others can also be beneficial when you are overwhelmed. If you lack someone to share the burden with, outsourcing or hiring a freelance contractor can save you time and effort.

✓ ***Focus on One Thing at a Time***
Multi-tasking can lead to decreased productivity and mental energy, which can be avoided by focusing on one project or task at a time. To be productive, you have to complete one task before moving on to the next item on your list.

✓ ***Block Time off on Your Calendar***
Calendaring events, meetings, deadlines and tasks saves time. Online apps like **Google Calendar** and **Calendly** help schedule time efficiently, allowing cross-device checking and reminder settings.

✓ *Limit Distractions*

Distractions from various sources, such as email, social media, friends and random thoughts, can hinder progress. To minimize these distractions, self-reflection and time management strategies can be employed, such as putting phones in different rooms, turning off notifications and blocking social media.

✓ *Summarize and Review Your Day*

End-of-day reflection is crucial for setting oneself up for success the next day. It involves reviewing to-do lists, identifying tasks completed and assessing time management. This process helps identify areas for improvement and improves overall performance.

➢ *Importance of Time Management*
- Increases productivity and efficiency.
- Reduces stress.
- Helps you to have a better control of your workflow.
- Increases the ability to consistently meet deadlines.
- Improves self-discipline.
- Provides a sense of fulfilment.
- Enhances decision-making abilities.
- Improves workplace relationships.
- Boosts your confidence.
- Produces quality work.

B. Money

Financial stability is important, but it is not the only indicator of wealth. Money should be used as a tool to achieve your goals and allow you to live the life you want. It is also crucial for you to understand that, without money, you will find it exceedingly difficult to have wealth and a decent life.

Do not be misled by the wrong interpretation some people have offered for **1 Timothy 6:10**, which says, "For the love of money is the root of all evil, which while some coveted after, they have erred from the faith and pierced themselves through with many sorrows." This verse does not show that money is bad; rather, it teaches you to pursue money with integrity and to never stray from your faith just because you have succeeded financially.

You should be diligent in your work and do everything you can to stay out of poverty. Keep in mind that all of the world's affluent people are not salary earners but rather salary payers. In other words, they are all business owners with multiple streams of income. Consider alternative legitimate strategies to increase your income, as outlined in **Chapter 5**. Study all the mediums for generating money discussed earlier and take action right away.

Finally, you must always strike a balance so that, while you seek money, other aspects of your life are not ignored. Have time for yourself, your family, and others.

C. Talents

Recognize and develop your unique abilities. Harnessing your talents produces fulfilment and contributes to your overall wealth. True wealth entails pursuing passions and discovering one's purpose. Identify the hobbies and interests that make you happy and fulfilled. Align your professional and financial objectives with your passions, skills and values. Engaging in meaningful and purposeful activities improves your enjoyment and boosts your likelihood of long-term success.

Talents play a significant role in wealth creation since they provide access to a wide range of opportunities. Unfortunately, many people refuse to develop their God-given talents, even when it is clear that they may achieve a lot with them without any struggle. Most parents have been brainwashed into believing that only education can alleviate poverty in their families.

Woe to you if you mention that you wish to pursue your talent or passion. Consider the current generation of footballers and athletes. The majority of them have told stories about how their parents shunned them for deciding to be footballers or athletes.

Parents prefer to invest resources in their children to take courses about which they know nothing and which may be irrelevant in their country or today's technology world. People have just refused to acknowledge that our world has evolved and that things are no longer the same as they once were. Consider the **pre- and post-COVID-19 pandemics**. Who would have anticipated that churches and companies would conduct their operations online? People are still working and obtaining degrees remotely and from the comfort of their own homes, and they are still accomplishing great results.

Kwame Yeboah, a talented Ghanaian multi-instrumentalist, had the privilege of performing before Queen Elizabeth II and Royal Family members in **2020**. He performed with his friend, who is popularly known as Craig David, at a Commonwealth Nations' celebration in **Buckingham Palace**. Kwame was the guitarist, while Craig David sang a powerful song. Kwame has also played guitar on significant international stages and events.

In March 2024, **Ghetto Kids**, who are dancers from Kampala, Uganda, and East Africa, were invited to perform at the Royal Commonwealth Service in London after they had previously performed on Britain's Got Talent in 2023.

I strongly believe Kwame and the Ghetto Kids went to school, but it was not their certificates; rather, it was their talents that took them to the palace.

The question is: How many academics or professors around the world have had the opportunity to appear at the aforementioned palace? The Bible says in **Proverbs 18:16, "A man's gift makes room for him and brings him before great men."** With your talent, you can also invent great things that do not exist, become wealthy and appear before kings and presidents in this world as those who receive formal education to the highest level. Formal education is valuable, but it should not come at the expense of our talents. We should maintain a sense of equilibrium in all parts of our lives.

You need to understand that there are major and significant changes in our world today and there are numerous technological ways of getting things done. With the introduction of **artificial intelligence (AI)** and **robotics**, you can have access to vast amounts of information without the need to visit a library before accessing it.

Artificial intelligence has advanced significantly in the field of medicine, including drug prescriptions. AI can help eliminate errors by offering accurate and reliable prescriptions. **GPT-3, created by OpenAI**, is an extremely sophisticated language model with 175 billion parameters. It can answer medical questions, diagnose illnesses and even prescribe medication.

Robots have been designed to talk accurately and can perform many of the tasks done by humans, including serving in restaurants. We should reconsider the courses we allow our children to take in school and the careers we choose for them and ourselves.

Most often, I hear individuals ask, **"How do we discover our talents?"**

Let's examine the following techniques for identifying talent:

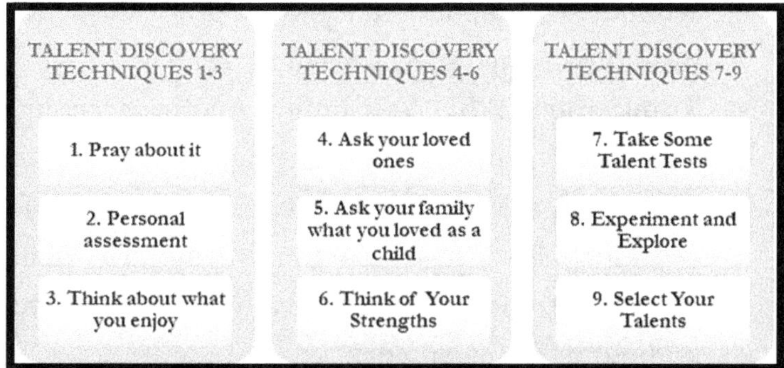

Figure 6.3

- **Pray about It:** We were all created by a superior deity, which I believe to be God. The creator understands you better than you do. He created and gave you life. God has gifted each of us with talents, so He is the best person to seek assistance in identifying your hidden talents. You must spend time in prayer and fasting to discover from your creator the type of assignment he has given you and the related talents. Uncovering your talents will allow you to avoid wasting your valuable time on activities that will not produce satisfactory outcomes for you.

- **Personal Assessment:** Apart from God, who created you, no one knows you better than you do. Take some time to reflect on your life, and you will notice that these are things you have done successfully before. These are the things you were good at but have since abandoned because of your chosen profession. These are the things you can perform without any guidance, and people were astounded, including trained specialists in those areas.

- **Think about What You Enjoy:** Another technique to discover your hidden talent is to start listing the things you enjoy doing and will not stop doing for anything else. These are things you love doing effortlessly, and you will be ready to do them even without receiving any pay.

- **Ask Your Loved Ones:** You can also discover your hidden talent by asking your close friends to list what your best and worst qualities are. They will genuinely list all of them for you. They can tell you that these are the things you are created to do because they may lack the talent to do them.

- **Ask Your Family What You Loved as a Child:** Your parents and siblings have spent many years with you and have much to say about you. You can simply find out from your parents and older siblings about the things you were interested in doing when growing up and the talent they discovered in you. You will be amazed by the details and evidence they will give you.

- **Think of Your Strengths:** You can also discover your hidden talent by finding out what makes you feel strong, what upsets you when you see people struggling to do something you can do with ease without thinking and getting bored, and what you can do better than almost everyone in your family, school, vicinity, or workplace.

- **Take Some Talent Tests:** You can also take a talent test that has been designed and structured to bring out the hidden talents in you. The test asks about your life experiences, skills, behaviors, cultural fits, and preferences to unravel your talents.

- **Experiment and Explore:** Try new stuff. Sometimes, we cannot explore our talents because we are locked in familiar routines. Attend seminars and conferences. Explore hobbies such as weaving, artwork, videography and athletics. You never know what will resonate with you. Use the internet to find inspiration. Platforms such as YouTube and Pinterest provide a variety of inspiration and creative activities.

- **Select Your Talents:** It is possible that you have multiple talents. You may excel at multiple things in life. And this might be a positive thing because it is highly motivating. During such moments, you must select from a list of things that you excel at. Determine what talent moves your heart and soul. What makes you happy and satisfied is what you should prioritize and seek. Simply choose and pursue your talent to live a happy and fulfilling life.

D. Prioritize Holistic Well-Being

Physical health and mental well-being are invaluable. Prioritize self-care, exercise and mental health. True wealth goes beyond financial achievement to encompass well-being. Prioritize your physical, mental and emotional well-being. Cultivate healthy habits such as exercise, decent nutrition and adequate sleep. Allow time for self-care, relaxation and mindfulness exercises. By taking care of your health, you lay the footing for a successful and meaningful life.

E. Wisdom

Continuous learning and personal improvement increase your wealth. Wisdom obtained through experiences and knowledge enriches your life. Knowledge is a powerful tool for increasing wealth. Take the time to learn about personal finances, investment strategies and the financial markets. Continuously seek opportunities to learn and remain relevant to market trends and changes. This knowledge will enable you to make better judgments and navigate the complexities of wealth creation more effectively. Now is the time to put your acquired knowledge into action, believe in your abilities, and take the necessary steps to change your financial future. Building wealth from nothing is indeed within your reach, and with determination and perseverance, you can manifest a life of financial freedom, security and lasting prosperity.

F. Networks and Community

Relationships are the foundation for true wealth. Make significant connections, give back to your community and enjoy the satisfaction of helping others. Wealth is more than just individual achievements; it also includes meaningful relationships. Develop and maintain ties with your family, friends and community. Invest time and effort in developing solid relationships based on trust, respect and support. Meaningful relationships can bring crucial assistance, happiness and a sense of belonging as you pursue your wealth-creation goals.

In conclusion, regularly evaluate your financial objectives, personal values and overall life satisfaction. Determine whether your wealth creation efforts are consistent with your desired results and values. Be flexible and change your methods and priorities as necessary. By constantly reflecting and modifying, you can ensure that your wealth creation journey aligns with your evolving goals and priorities.

Remember that it is more than just amassing wealth; it is about living a balanced, fulfilling life in which relationships and personal growth play an important role.

Chapter 7|
Levels of Wealth

These levels provide a framework for understanding your current financial situation and what it takes to progress to the next level. These levels measure your growth from dependence level to abundance level. They provide a more basic assessment of your financial journey. Understanding your wealth level aids in making informed decisions about investments, savings and retirement planning, promoting a secure and happier future. **There are several levels of wealth.** However, we can classify them all into seven major levels.

The seven (7) Levels of Wealth discuss the concept of financial security, highlighting the importance of understanding your current financial situation and setting realistic goals. Study the levels carefully and compare them to your financial situation to know exactly where you are. Knowing your current level will help you ascertain if you are on the right path and if not, you should make the necessary adjustments to realize your financial goal. Remember that there is no shortcut to achieving your financial objectives. Exercise patience and discipline, and be committed to your goals. Also, learn from those who have attained the level you aspire to, and everything will be well for you. Now, let's explore the seven levels of wealth below:

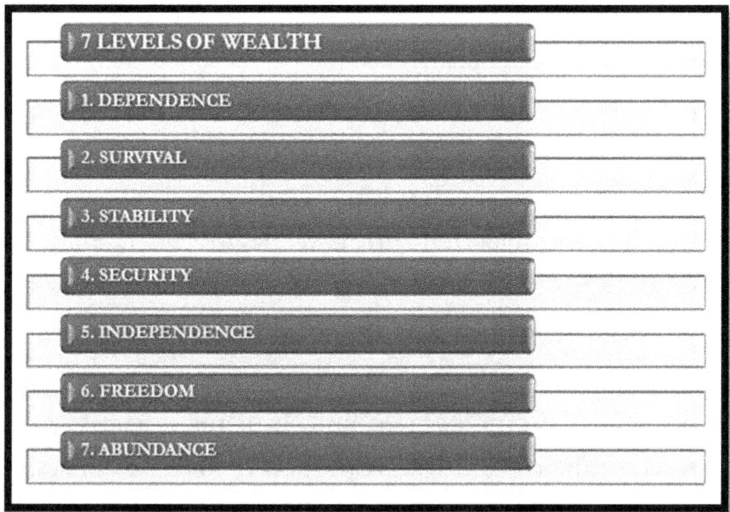

Figure 7.1

Here are the seven levels:

➤ *Dependence*

This is the first level. At this level, you still rely on someone else to provide for you. If you are a young child, this is perfectly fine. But if you are an adult, you generally do not want to stay at this level for very long. Most adults would be dissatisfied to remain at this level.

Unfortunately, many of us have encountered this situation at some point in our lives due to unforeseen events. This can depend on 'the state' or on our family. When this happens in adulthood, money is not simply on your mind; it appears to be the only thing on your mind. At this level, there is practically no source of income, leaving you vulnerable and dependent on others or your loved ones for your basic necessities.

When you remain at this level for an extended period of time, you will feel frustrated and develop an inferiority complex. The individual providing support eventually becomes fed up and begins to display an adverse disposition toward you.

Furthermore, this is the level at which you will be subjected to increased pressure and are frequently forced to work in menial employment and, in some circumstances, engage in illicit activities. You should make a conscious effort not to return to this level if feasible because it is an unpleasant level to be at.

➢ *Survival*

You earn sufficient income to cover your expenses. You can pay all of your expenses or debts, but there are not enough funds left for savings. Nonetheless, you no longer need someone to financially support you. At the same time, other people live a glamorous lifestyle but find themselves stuck at this level. Even if they drive a great vehicle and wear nice clothes, they can be one paycheck away from financial ruin.

You are not financially stable if you are at this level, but you can provide for your basic needs and are not dependent on others. You should focus on your basic needs rather than their wants if you are at this level. You should also look for alternative ways to increase your earnings. You can work part-time or do something profitable on the weekends, such as petty trading. At this level, there should be no pressure on you to earn more money than others, and there is no need to create comparisons between yourself and others. Simply work hard and keep your speed.

> *Stability*

You consistently make enough money to pay your expenses and still have sufficient funds to begin saving. You have at least six months' worth of living expenses in your contingency fund, so if you lose your job, which is the principal source of your income, you still have six months to get back on track. You can also manage your debt efficiently and repay your loans on time.

At this stage, your financial stress levels start to diminish. You can start saving money for your future, although it is only a small amount. You do have some assets that you are developing; perhaps you have been able to get on the property ladder. The primary emphasis must be on the present moment.

This is the most deceptive level since numerous people assume they have arrived merely because they have a regular income. They revert to dependence if they are dismissed without sufficient compensation or a redundancy package.

Most people at this level believe they will always be employed and can save at any time because they have more years to retire. Unfortunately, some believe they are indispensable and, as a result, refuse to set aside money for savings or unforeseen costs.

> ➤ *Security*

With a regular income and sufficient savings, you can now focus on building wealth and planning for retirement. The extra funds you currently have can be invested in securities that are appropriate for your risk tolerance and financial objectives. The more money you set aside for the correct investments, the faster you will achieve your objectives. At this level, you are satisfied with the safety and security that the money provides.

At this level, your financial status appears to have improved significantly. You have up to a year of emergency savings in cash and a significant amount saved for the future. You are certain that if you had a problem at work or an unexpected expense, you would be able to handle it.

Your improved financial condition has altered your perspective on life slightly. You are now looking forward to your profession and life rather than just putting bread on the table. Simply put, you have begun to expand the luxury of choice, and the idea of taking a risk no longer appears to be completely out of reach. At this level, you are not experiencing daily financial anxiety but are concerned about the future and whether you can afford to achieve your goals. Despite being financially better than others, you still have significant questions about your financial future and whether you can afford to provide your family with the life they desire.

➢ *Independence*

You have been investing continuously for several years and have an investment portfolio and long-term assets that provide you with enough passive income to support your day-to-day living needs in retirement. This effectively means that you do not have to work another day in your life if you don't want to; you can now fund your daily needs with your money without stress.

At this level, you have great control over your financial situation. You no longer rely on a single source of income and have a diverse portfolio.

At this level, you have achieved financial independence by earning sufficient income and living off your assets. However, you still want to continue working, as your concept of work has changed. Your time has become an asset, but you still feel unfulfilled by spending all your days on the games of your choice. The habits needed to achieve this independence have taken time to instill.

➢ *Freedom*

At this level, you continue to increase your resources to the point where your assets and passive income can easily fund your desired lifestyle. You now have the means to pursue your dreams and aspirations, including global travel, luxury items and unique experiences.

This is a level that many people aspire to, but only a few can achieve. You have substantial financial freedom. Work becomes optional, and you can pursue passions or interests without financial constraints.

> ➢ *Abundance*

At this level, your primary focus is on being a proper steward of your money and leaving behind your legacy for future generations, as you have more than you will ever need.

At this level, you have abundant resources and can focus on your legacy. Reflect on your impact on the world and your ability to pass on skills. However, you question whether you used your time wisely and made better decisions.

Remember that happiness is not solely tied to wealth. While financial stability is essential, finding contentment and purpose in life goes beyond money. Each person's journey through these levels is unique, and it is perfectly fine to find happiness at any stage.

Chapter 8|
Wealth and Mindset

Many people dream of wealth, but unfortunately, they have not developed the right financial mindset. A mindset is a set of ideas, attitudes, beliefs and actions that inform your thoughts and decisions about something.

Mindset can also be seen as the lens through which we see the world, shaping our beliefs, perceptions and attitudes. They can either obscure or clear our path and adopting a healthy wealth mindset helps us achieve our financial goals and earn more money.

It is this mindset that distinguishes the wealthy from others. A financial mindset will help you make the most of your money, but it does not come easily. A financial mindset helps you spend less, make prudent investments, and look for ways to enhance your financial situation with low risk.

It will be extremely challenging for a person to achieve financial freedom unless they have the proper mindset. This is true because our actions are based on what we have previously considered and planned in our minds. Everything we do as humans is the result of our thoughts or mindsets. Creating an effective financial strategy necessitates the appropriate mindset. Building a mindset that considers financial security goes beyond just money.

True financial freedom requires a combination of knowledge, discipline and mindset.

Cultivating a healthy mindset is crucial for success, as it helps stick to financial goals and enhances earning potential.

The key to developing the right mindset is understanding that financial planning is a journey requiring flexibility, adaptability and determination. Despite obstacles, stay focused, open to learning, and seek professional advice when needed.

Have you ever wondered why some people seem to effortlessly amass wealth while others struggle to make ends meet? Is it luck or destiny? Or is it something entirely else? "Many believe that the answer lies not in the size of one's bank account but in the mindset. Some argue that a wealthy mindset is the real key to financial success. But how does the mindset of the wealthy differ from that of the average person?"

Firstly, let's consider **the concept of risk**. The average person tends to avoid risk. They seek security and stability. They put their money in savings accounts. They have worked the same job for years and follow the tried-and-true path. The wealthy, on the other hand, embrace risk. They see it not as a danger but as an opportunity. They invest in securities, start businesses and take chances. Also, they understand that without risk, there can be no reward.

Secondly, let us consider **the idea of work**. For the average person, work is a means to an end. It is a way to earn a paycheck and pay bills. But for the wealthy, work is a passion. It is a way to create, innovate, and make a difference. They do not work for money; they work for the joy of it. And since they love what they do, they are willing to put in the hours, effort, sweat and tears that success requires.

Lastly, let's look at the **concept of money itself**. The average person sees money as a scarce resource. They believe there is only that much to go around, and they have to fight for their share. The wealthy, however, see money as abundant. They know there is enough for everyone, and they are not afraid to share their wealth. They invest in others and donate to charity. They also use their money to make the world a better place.

So, what does all this mean? It suggests that wealth is not just about money but also about mindset. It is about how you view risk, work and money. The good news is that these are all things that can be changed. You can learn to embrace risk, find the work you love, see money as abundant and develop a wealthy mindset.

> ➢ *How to Develop a Wealthy Mindset?*

A wealthy mindset goes beyond financial strategies; it involves cultivating a positive and abundant outlook on life.

People frequently generalize prosperity, but actual wealth is unattainable owing to a mindset that keeps them from thinking wealthy, trapping them in mediocrity and victimization.

Now, let's look at the ways below for developing a wealthy mindset.

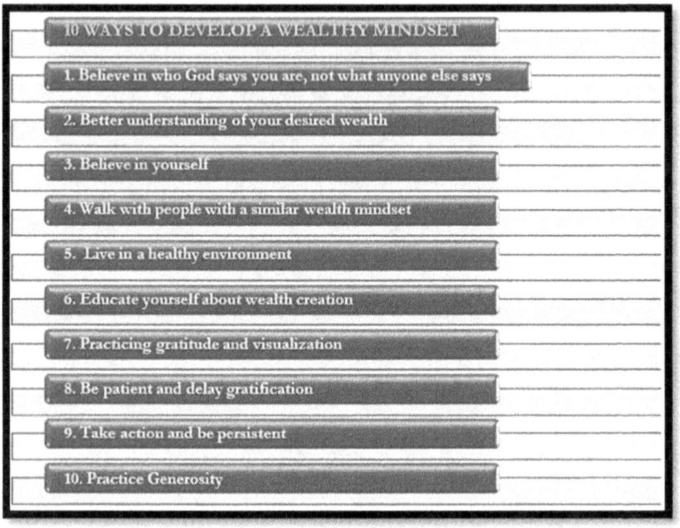

Figure 8.1

- **Believe in Who God Says You Are, Not What Anyone Else Says:** God wants us to appreciate the abundance of His kindness. Adam and Eve discovered a rich land in the magnificent Garden of Eden, and humanity was designed to thrive in every aspect. God provides plenty of resources and chances for mankind to flourish.

  This is God's will for your life, as correctly highlighted in **3 John 2, "Beloved, I wish above all things that thou mayest prosper and be in health, even as thy soul prospereth."**

You should have the mindset that you are wealthy and prosperous. Whenever others call you wealthy, please embrace it, even if things are not moving the way you want.

- **Better Understanding of Your Desired Wealth:** People often believe that being wealthy means you should at least have some real estate, investments, businesses and multiple streams of income. Also, being wealthy means you should have a sound, comfortable and impactful life. These are people's assessments of what a wealthy person should possess.

  However, it is important to have a personal understanding of how you perceive wealth and the kind of wealth that you desire and want to generate for yourself. You cannot create wealth if you do not subscribe to it. Defining your understanding of wealth can help you make better financial decisions and take effective measures that will enable you to achieve your desired wealth.

- **Believe in Yourself:** Once you have a clear grasp of your desired wealth, you must implement effective strategies to acquire it. You need to believe in yourself and stick to your ideas. People do not need to believe in you or your perception of wealth because we all have our own perspectives and views. Do not expect them to embrace your definition of wealth so simply. You must believe that you will become wealthy and remain optimistic about it, regardless of the circumstances. Do not let others impose their perceptions and opinions on you.

- **Walk with People with a Similar Wealth Mindset:** Surround yourself with individuals with similar wealth perspectives to influence your mindset and life experiences. You have to avoid discrimination and at the same time, be mindful of who you associate with.

  However, associating with like-minded individuals can lead to prosperity, as they offer encouragement and advice. People who lack ambition and have a negative wealth mindset might quickly infect you with their lethal disease of mediocrity.

  The law of attraction works perfectly in this case. Negative wealth mindsets attract mediocrity, while positive mindsets produce positive outcomes.

- **Live in a Healthy Environment:** A healthy environment fosters a wealth mindset, encouraging harmonious living with wealthy individuals, fostering business connections, and promoting a wealth mindset essential for wealth accumulation. Your mindset and behaviors may be influenced by an unhealthy environment where individuals criticize the wealthy and have a negative perception of wealth.

- **Educate Yourself about Wealth Creation:** To develop a wealth mindset, invest in yourself and educate yourself on financial intelligence, integrity and independence. Learn about passive income, investing, and budgeting to create the wealth you need. This mindset ensures your actions align with your financial goals, leading to success.

- **Practising Gratitude and Visualization:** Embrace gratitude for resources and opportunities obtained; practise daily gratitude to reset your mind from being poor to wealthy; and use visualization techniques to picture your financial goals being realized, fostering belief in their attainability.

- **Be Patient and Delay Gratification:** The issue of instant gratification, known as PIG, is when individuals prioritize small rewards over larger ones, leading to addiction and a lack of self-discipline, akin to crack cocaine.

  Rewarding your actions triggers a surge of feel-good hormones, causing a lot of excitement. However, those with a healthy relationship with money and abundant thinking habits understand the importance of delaying gratification. Instead of focusing on the present, start planning for the future and say no to instant gratification.

- **Take Action and Be Persistent:** A wealth mindset involves positive thinking, persistent action, resilience, and adaptability in pursuing financial goals despite initial setbacks, as well as focusing on the end goal.

- **Practise Generosity:** Real wealth involves more than just financial success; it also involves you participating in acts of generosity and positively influencing others to draw even more wealth into your life.

In summary, the mindset of the wealthy differs significantly from that of the average person. The wealthy embrace risk, see work as a passion and view money as abundant. The average person, on the other hand, avoids risk, sees work as a means to an end, and views money as scarce. But remember, these are not fixed traits. They are attitudes, beliefs and perspectives, and they can be changed. So, the question is not about whether or not you are wealthy, but rather, whether you have a wealthy mindset. Also, remember that it is not about the money in your bank account but the thoughts in your head. This is a wealthy mindset and a prosperous future.

"What the mind can conceive and believe it can achieve."

— ***Napoleon Hill***

Chapter 9|
Wealth and Information

Information is simply knowledge obtained from investigation, study, or instruction. It can also be referred to as facts or processed data.

Information is an essential component of our daily lives, penetrating multiple fields. Whether for personal growth, economic progress, or decision-making, access to relevant and reliable information is essential.

In today's fast-paced, ever-changing world, the need for information has grown even stronger. Information has become a new form of wealth. It is not just about the traditional forms of wealth we are familiar with, such as money, property, or gold. In the digital age, access to the right information can open doors to opportunities, influence and power.

Consider this: the most valuable companies in the world today are not those that mine for gold or drill for oil. They are the tech giants who have mastered the art of extracting, analyzing and leveraging user data.

They have turned information into their most valuable asset and built empires around it.

Think about Google, a company that began as a simple search engine. Now, it is a multinational corporation that knows what you are searching for, what you are interested in, and even where you have been. It mines and processes this information, turning it into a product that advertisers are eager to buy. It is not just Google but Facebook, Amazon, and Apple—they have all recognized the value of information and have become masters at gathering and using it to their advantage.

These tech giants have built their wealth on information, proving that knowledge truly is power in the modern world. However, it is not just big corporations that can benefit from this new form of wealth. Common people like you and me can also harness the power of information. With access to the internet, we can learn new skills, stay informed about world events, and make informed decisions that can lead to personal and financial growth. So, the next time you log onto your computer, remember that the information you are accessing and the data you are creating are all valuable.

It is a new form of wealth that, when utilized correctly, can lead to great opportunities and power. "In the digital era, information is indeed power, and power translates to wealth."
Individuals and companies must have access to cutting-edge research, trends, and ideas to remain competitive and relevant.

Information is very important when it comes to wealth creation. Many investors rely heavily on both qualitative and quantitative information to make informed decisions about their investments and businesses. It will be extremely difficult to safeguard your wealth without properly having access to reliable information.

Though information is important in wealth creation, you should be extremely careful with the source of the information and must always take steps to verify it before making any decision. You must be especially concerned about the operations and performance of the investment company where you are currently saving or investing. You can sign up for news bulletins from your investment company and always monitor the performance of your savings or investments.

It is important to note that some people have become wealthy and successful investors not because of their money but simply because they had access to vital information that they capitalized on for investment, which yielded a lot of returns for them.

I also know individuals who, after receiving reliable information about investment prospects, contacted their banks for a loan that was approved, and their wealth value increased as a result of the investment.

Furthermore, many investors' investments and savings were safeguarded when they discovered trustworthy information concerning the bad performance of their investment managers and the overall security market. With this information, they promptly redeemed their investments, even though they had not matured. It was prudent for them to pay a penalty for early redemption rather than lose the entire investment.

You may be aware that the foreign exchange market is subject to frequent fluctuations, having a significant impact on many businesses and individuals. The question is: How do these organizations and people mitigate the possible risk of currency exchange fluctuations? Most of those that require currency to operate monitor the forex market and consult with their bankers or consultants for updates. When they receive credible information that the local currency will appreciate against foreign currencies, they promptly accumulate additional local cash to acquire foreign currencies as soon as there is a dip. Others use forwards, futures, swaps, and option contracts to hedge against the risk of FX fluctuations.

> ➢ *The Interplay of Wealth and Information*

Now, let's look at the interplay of wealth and information.

Let's take a step back to see the big picture. Imagine the world as a massive checkerboard. The pieces represent wealth, whereas the rules represent information. Wealth moves based on information in the same way as pieces move according to the rules.

However, not all players comprehend the rules the same way. This is known as 'information asymmetry'. Certain individuals have a distinct advantage because they have access to more information than others.

This information can take many forms, such as a tip about a new start-up that is ready to take off or an anticipated policy change that will shake up a sector. Those who have access to such vital information can make sound decisions about where to invest their money, frequently resulting in significant gains.

However, it is not entirely one-way traffic. Wealth might also affect access to information. The wealthier a person, the more resources they can devote to gathering information. They can employ financial experts, pay for premium news services, or even conduct their own research. Furthermore, wealth can also generate information. A wealthy individual making a substantial investment has the potential to affect market trends by producing new information to which others can react. So, in essence, wealth and information exist in a symbiotic relationship. Information shapes the distribution of wealth, while wealth determines access to information. It is a cycle that is constantly in motion, with each aspect influencing and being influenced by the other.

The interplay between information and wealth can perpetuate wealth inequality, as those with access to information can increase their wealth, while those without access may find themselves left behind. Yet, the cycle is not unbreakable. Financial literacy, a form of information itself, can help level the playing field, providing individuals with the knowledge to make savvy financial decisions regardless of their initial wealth.

> *Financial Information*

Now, let's look at financial information, which is very useful in decision-making and has a significant impact on a person's wealth.

Financial information refers to information concerning a person's or a company's monetary transactions. Financial information includes reports and data that provide stakeholders with insight into a firm's financial performance. Stakeholders, such as regulators, employees, management, investors or shareholders, creditors or suppliers, customers, and government, use this information to make informed financial decisions.

Creditors and lenders use this information to determine credit risk. Financial information includes credit or debit card numbers, credit ratings from third-party credit analysis agencies, financial documents and payment histories.

Anyone who uses financial information has a responsibility to keep the information secure, as it can be exploited by third parties to commit identity theft.

Financial information is often summarized in an organization's financial statements, which are then reviewed by financial statement users to determine the reporting entity's financial position, income statement and cash flows.

In the context of wealth creation, financial information can be used in the following ways:

- **Business Operations Decision-Making**. A company's owners utilize financial data to decide whether to make adjustments to operations, such as investing in particular product lines, closing others, scaling back recruiting, and so on.

- **Credit Lending Decision-Making**. Lenders and creditors use financial information to determine if a business or individual is able to repay a loan or pay an invoice. Updates to financial information can be used to restrict existing credit or loans.

- **Investment Decision-Making:** Financial information is used by investors to determine whether to invest in a firm or sell their stake in an existing business.
- **Risk Management:** Risk management is crucial for investors and management to control risk and make informed investment decisions, relying on authentic corporate financial information.
- **Diversification:** Financial information allows investors to diversify their investments by investing in various investment portfolios.

In business, there are **two main stakeholders: internal** and **external.** Internal stakeholders, such as directors, managers and employees, are part of the company, while external stakeholders, like shareholders or investors, creditors or suppliers, customers, regulators, and the government, are not. Their evaluation through financial information such as financial statements is crucial.

❖ *Users or Stakeholders of Financial Information*

Let's now look at the various users or stakeholders of financial information and how they utilize that information.

✓ **Lenders**

They are the providers of funding and must be fully informed about the firm's financial position through financial statements, the auditor's report and market analysis to ensure a comprehensive understanding. They also endeavor to comprehend individual financial situations from the information provided on their forms before deciding on the amount to lend to them.

✓ *Regulators*

They are regulatory bodies that mandate businesses to provide financial reports, oversee the compliance process, and enforce industry and business regulations. They issue licenses to entities that fit under their mandate. They require financial information to assess the companies' performance and determine whether or not they are consistently satisfying the capital requirements and other conditions imposed on them.

Regulators include the Securities Exchange Commission (SEC) and Central Banks from various countries.

✓ *Directors and Managers*

Directors are senior management positions that supervise various aspects of an organization. Directors are hired and directly accountable to key stakeholders. Managers are professionals who oversee particular areas or departments within an organization.

They require financial information for the following:

- To establish overall objectives and periodical targets.
- To assess the results of the policies implemented, whether they are having any positive effect, and plan for future expansion and investments.

- To avoid dissimulations and corruption.
- To establish squired systems and strengthen control of procedures.
- To increase the productivity level of the organization.
- To make decisions about new investments, project appreciation, and continued and discontinued operations.
- To make dividend decisions.
- To make diversified business decisions.
- To make winding up decision.

✓ *Shareholders*

A shareholder is any individual or corporation that owns shares in a company. A company shareholder can own as little as one can share. When shareholders sell their shares, they realize capital gains or losses and may earn dividends if the company pays them. Shareholders have certain privileges, such as voting at shareholder meetings to approve board members, dividend distributions and mergers. In the event of bankruptcy, stockholders may lose up to their entire investment.

Shareholders require financial information for the following:

- To determine whether their investment will be sold, diluted or bought by the organization.
- To decide whether to invest their funds in the business and the level of return that they can expect from the investments.

- To determine the fairness of the returns for their investments.
- To ascertain the going concern of the organization.
- To obtain broad knowledge about organizational activities.
- To compare their investments and their benefits with other competitive organizations and industries.

✓ *Employees*

Employees are paid workers who work for a company, either full-time or part-time and are compensated by the employer. Simply put, they are the workers of an organization.

They require financial information for the following:
- To know about the stability and profitability of the employer.
- To know about remuneration, retirement benefits and employment opportunities in the organization.
- To ensure the job security with the current employer.
- To ensure the fairness of the salaries and wages they obtain from the organization according to their earnings.
- To have a clear view of other operations of the organization.

✓ *Suppliers*

A supplier is a business entity or individual that supplies goods and services, contributing significantly to a product's value, either as a manufacturer, distributor, or service provider.

They require financial information for the following:

- To ensure their payments of supplies are received on due.
- To ensure the stability of their customers.
- To have knowledge about other products and their suppliers of the organization.
- To compare their transaction with existing and other companies.
- To find other competitive suppliers and their contribution towards the organization.
- To find opportunities to supply more.

✓ *Customer*

A customer is an individual or entity that purchases goods or services from another person or company, driving revenues and ensuring the survival and growth of the company.

They require financial information for the following:

- To have knowledge about the cost structure of the products that the organization is producing.
- To ensure the stability of the organization.

- To know about the organization's profitability because profitability sheds light on products, possible growth, improvements, best customer service and low price strategic implications.
- To know about CSR programs conducted by the organization.

✓ *Government*

A government is a system or group of people that governs a state. It consists of three branches: legislation, executive, and judiciary, and it can take various forms, including democracies, totalitarian regimes, and monarchies.

The government requires financial information for the following:

- To collect accurate taxes and amounts from organizations on due dates.
- To provide government benefaction to improve their business.
- To obtain financial and non-financial assistance for government development projects.
- To ensure the organizations oversee their employees in a reasonable way.
- To ensure that the organizations comply with the rules, regulations and acts established by the government.

❖ *Sources of Financial Information for Investors*

Financial information sources are channels for obtaining data, facts and insights, encompassing various mediums and formats. They shape your understanding of the various financial and investment issues, contribute to decision-making, and have expanded in the digital age. There are many sources from which investors can obtain reliable information to guide them in their decision-making process. Below are some of the sources from which investors can obtain useful financial information:

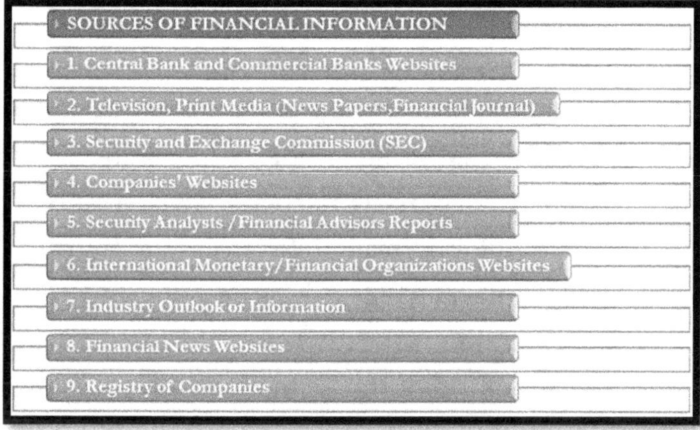

Figure 9.1

✓ ***Central Bank and Commercial Banks' Websites***

The Central Bank is the nation's primary monetary authority. It regulates and supervises financial institutions, manages the national currency and implements monetary policy. It is also responsible for issuing operating licenses to commercial banks and other financial institutions. Investors can find the latest news, exchange rates, inflation rates, relevant financial reports, publications, and much more on its home pages. Fortunately, it also publishes commercial banks and financial institutions in good standing on its websites.

As an investor, you must also carry out due diligence on these banks and financial institutions before saving or investing with them. One of the easiest ways is to check the central bank's website to see if they are in good standing and if they always meet the minimum capital requirements of the central bank.

Furthermore, having satisfied yourself that the bank or financial institution you intend to save or invest with is in good standing and meets the central bank's minimum capital requirements, the next thing to do is to visit that bank's website to analyze its financial statements, reports and other relevant information to ascertain its financial performance before making a decision. However, if you cannot carry out this due diligence, it is important to contact a financial advisor for the necessary advice or assistance.

✓ *Television, Print Media (News Papers, Financial Journals & Magazines)*

Financial information regarding businesses and investments is widely available through various media outlets, including television, the Internet, newspapers, and financial publications. Although this information can help investors forecast investment returns and business success or failure, not everyone understands it. Mass media has long been used to disseminate vital information, elicit emotion, provide advice, and broadcast significant news. Business news and channels provide excellent updates and analyst perspectives, but caution should be exercised when relying on the information provided.

✓ *Security and Exchange Commission (SEC)*

The SEC regulates and promotes the growth and development of an efficient, fair, and transparent securities market while protecting investors and the market's integrity. The SEC registers, licenses, approves or regulates in accordance with existing Acts or Regulations. It monitors license holders' solvency and takes steps to protect clients' interests when a license holder's solvency is in doubt. It also monitors securities transactions to ensure that they are orderly, fair and equitable. Finally, it formulates principles to guide the sector.

The SEC oversees the establishment of securities exchanges, commodities and future exchanges, securities depositories, clearing institutions, credit rating agencies, fund managers, investment advisers, unit trusts, mutual funds and other securities businesses.

Just as we have in many countries, the Securities and Exchange Commission mandates all publicly traded companies to report their financial information, and foreign companies listed on the exchanges must also do so annually.

Investors who are willing to trade in both money and capital market products must first visit the SEC website to have access to their annual reports, public notices, press releases and other information. They will also have access to a published list of all entities that have been licensed in different categories to undertake the mandated activities. This due diligence by investors is very crucial for their decision-making regarding investments and arrangements.

✓ *Companies' Websites*

Companies' websites offer a wealth of information about the company, including financial statements, annual reports, news, press releases and financial presentations. They are a reliable source of information, especially international information, which they usually give to shareholders that are not covered in SEC filings. They provide a wealth of content, making it easier to access financial data than through government agencies.

Financial statements of companies provide crucial information on a company's financial stability, including the balance sheet, income statement and statement of cash flows, which summarize assets, liabilities, equity, revenues, expenses and cash generation.

In addition to the information obtained on the SEC website, investors must conduct due diligence on companies' websites, read about their activities, directors and managers, and analyze their financial reports and other relevant information before buying shares or investing in the company.

✓ *Security Analysts/Financial Advisors' Reports*

Analysts' reports are opinions on a company's current and future performance, but they can be biased. It is important to use other sources to confirm these opinions. Financial websites like Morningstar and Yahoo Finance provide these reports, while stockbrokers may offer in-house research or subscribe to third-party analysts. Securities analysts focusing on selling investments can be useful but should be used with caution. Buy-side analysts working for mutual funds or investment institutions are also good sources but may not be widely available.

✓ *International Monetary/Financial Organizations Websites, e.g. IMF, World Bank*

The International Monetary Fund (IMF) is a global organization aiming for sustainable growth and prosperity for its 190 member countries. It supports economic policies promoting financial stability, monetary cooperation and productivity. The IMF monitors currencies, promotes global economic growth and addresses poverty.

On the other hand, The World Bank Group, established in 1944, complements the efforts of the International Monetary Fund (IMF) by providing financial and technical assistance to developing countries, focusing on poverty reduction and economic development.

International financial organizations provide global financial advice and directives, providing updates on monetary matters that may impact investments. Investors can anticipate recessions or economic crunches by following these organizations, ensuring they are aware of potential economic changes.

✓ *Industry Outlook/Information*

Industry outlook magazines and online trade journals provide insights into industry activity and health. Investment decisions should consider market demand, capacity utilization, market share, market leaders, prospects, international demand, labor issues and government policy towards the industry.

✓ *Financial News Websites*

Websites like **Yahoo Finance**, **Bloomberg and Vanguard** offer real-time financial news, stock prices and market insights for investors and individuals.

Yahoo Finance is a valuable resource for new investors, offering comprehensive information on retirement planning, college funding, credit, personal finance and stock market growth. It features calculators for retirement income and mortgage costs.

Bloomberg Terminals provides professional traders with financial information, while its minimalist website offers news, equities, and up-to-date information for European companies.

Vanguard is known for its low-cost investment approach and provides valuable information and education for beginners, including financial calculators for determining retirement savings.

Investors can access more information on investment products by visiting the websites mentioned above.

✓ *Registry of Companies*

A registry of companies is a legal entity mandated to register, dissolve, determine representation, protect, and control legal entities. It is appointed according to established laws. A registry of companies can provide investors with valuable information regarding the incorporation of the company, the activities it is registered to carry out, and whether the company is still in operation.

❖ *Evaluation of Investment Information Sources*

Despite numerous reliable sources of investment information, verifying high-quality sources is crucial for investors to make informed decisions about a company. Investors should use the three criteria mentioned below to verify any source of investment information.

✓ *Reliability*

Investors should verify the accuracy, completeness and lack of bias of information sources, avoiding ambiguous, prejudiced or misleading ones.

✓ *Relevance*

Relevance in information is determined by its alignment with an investor's objectives, risk tolerance, and investment timeframe. Investors and creditors should select sources that align with their specific investment focus and avoid irrelevant information.

✓ *Timeliness*

Timeliness in investment information refers to its frequency of updates and speed in reflecting market changes, ensuring investors and creditors use current and precise sources.

In summary, understanding the value of information, capitalizing on its potential and effectively integrating it can pave the path for wealth creation in our interconnected world. Make use of your available resources, seek advice from financial specialists or mentors who specialize in wealth-building, use online tools and technology to manage your finances and find investment opportunities.

Chapter 10|
Wealth and Health

When health fails, wealth becomes useless, and when wealth is scarce, health deteriorates. Consequently, there is a significant relationship between the two. Poor financial insecurity leads to mental stress, reduced productivity, and job performance, while poor physical health directly impacts financial stability, increasing the likelihood of personal bankruptcy.

Figure 10.1

We frequently hear people say that health is wealth, implying that you can only labor to acquire wealth if you are healthy and have a sound mind. As a result, health is regarded as the most precious asset that a person may possess.

It is critical that you prioritize your health when attaining wealth. Otherwise, you risk losing the fortunes you have worked so hard to earn while battling for your health.

Unfortunately, several wealthy individuals had become incredibly destitute as a result of an unforeseen chronic illness that had dissipated all of their previously earned resources.

Good health means not only the absence of maladies in an individual's body but also the complete physical, mental, social and spiritual well-being of that individual.

The most pitiful aspect of life is being able to accumulate so much wealth and then be unable to enjoy it due to disease. People who did not sow will now reap the accumulated wealth and may even overlook your children's needs. You must stay healthy and put your house in order for a number of reasons outlined earlier.

Health, regarded as the most valuable asset, provides you with the most desired satisfaction, enjoyment and peaceful mind to enjoy the wealth acquired.

Regular health and wealth check-ups are crucial for personal and financial security, as amassing wealth without good health is meaningless. To evaluate your health and wealth on an annual basis, consult with the right experts and act on their advice.

Health and wealth are essential for a good life, as bad health can lead to premature mortality and high medical costs. Adopting healthy practices extends life expectancy and necessitates a greater retirement balance. Health, financial stability, work and family relationships are all factors that contribute to happiness.

A healthier lifestyle involves eating right, exercising regularly, avoiding drugs, alcohol, and too much sugar and salt, getting enough sleep, exercising and avoiding stressful situations. Wealthy individuals enjoy better living conditions and healthcare, reducing their risk of chronic illness, while poverty and social inequalities can lead to poor healthcare, low birth weight and developmental defects.

All things being equal, wealthier individuals can live longer, have fewer chronic diseases and maintain higher function into old age, with reduced death rates and lower risk of lifestyle conditions.

The deep connection between health and wealth necessitates the development and implementation of strategies to effectively manage both for life-enhancing benefits and opportunities.

In summary, the relationship between health and wealth is intricate, with both dimensions significantly impacting each other. Balancing these is crucial for overall well-being and prosperity. Wealth usually dominates our lives and determines our status, access to resources, and happiness.

It provides comfort, education and lifestyle luxuries, whereas health is the cornerstone of life. Wealth can bring happiness and possibilities, but without health, wealth can be meaningless.

The key to happiness is to strike a balance between wealth and health, realizing that wealth is more than just amassing money; it is also about using it wisely to better our lives and the lives of people around us. Maintaining excellent health involves nurturing our physical, mental and emotional well-being rather than avoiding disease.

Chapter 11|
Entrepreneurship and Wealth Creation

Entrepreneurship is the process of starting and running a business for profit. It significantly promotes economic growth and development in both developed and developing countries. It fosters job creation, innovation and market competition, benefiting consumers. Understanding the intricacies of entrepreneurial ventures is crucial, as successful ventures can significantly impact one's wealth.

As we have already discussed in the preceding chapters, the wealthiest people in the world today are those who own multibillion-dollar companies. These include Amazon, Facebook, Oracle, Tesla, Microsoft, Ali Express, Dangote Cement, and oil refineries.

It is also important to mention that the above-mentioned companies were started small by their owners and gradually flourished to become what we see today. As an upcoming entrepreneur, you need to be aware that successful businesses take time to build, and there are many obstacles in the journey of entrepreneurship. Do not be discouraged by naysayers and mistakes, but be patient, learn from the successful ones, and keep your pace. It will surely end in victory.

It is evident that for you to be financially successful, you have to think of entrepreneurship. However, it is important to mention that it is not an easy journey, as it involves a lot of risks. These risks should not be a discouraging factor, as, with the right strategies, an entrepreneur can easily mitigate the potential risks.

Many people began their own businesses, but regrettably, they failed due to a lack of understanding of how to run a profitable firm. Many people do not take the time to learn more about the type of business they wish to start. Others copy blindly without first knowing the stories of the entrepreneurs they are copying from, hence the failure.

If you want to undertake a new business, it is important for you to answer certain kinds of questions before you start the business. Please document your answers, as they will be your guide throughout the entire process of starting your business. There is a popular saying that if you **"fail to plan, you will plan to fail."** This conveys a straightforward message that not preparing adequately for a task or situation ultimately leads to failure. In other words, when you neglect to make proper plans, you inadvertently set yourself up for unsuccessful outcomes.

Planning is very important at the initial stage before the business kicks off. That is why a lot of people normally prepare a business plan before the start of the business. Similarly, by jotting down the answers to the below questions, you are indirectly preparing a brief business plan for your business. As much as possible, I will be expounding on each of the questions listed.

Let's now look at them in detail:

> ### *What Kind of Business Should I Do?*

This question requires you to do a critical study of the numerous business ideas you have. To be able to choose the right one, you should first be able to identify the type of problem that your company will be tackling. This will help you determine whether your company will survive or not. You can create a small questionnaire or conduct small oral interviews at the place where you wish to operate your business to learn about the kind of problems the people there are experiencing and whether your company is the solution provider. Remember, people will only pay for solutions to their problems. For example, if individuals in your area commute or walk a significant distance to acquire food or water, you can open a restaurant or water business to meet their needs.

> ### *What Permit or Certification Is Required for the Chosen Business?*

You need to do some research to find out the kind of permit or certification required before starting your business.

In most countries, before you can operate a business, you need to register your business with the government authority responsible for business registration for a certificate of incorporation and a tax identification number (TIN). You may decide to register your company as a sole proprietorship (one-man business), partnership, or a limited liability company.

In addition to the above registration, you may also be required to obtain other permits, depending on the business you want to operate. Food and water businesses require a Food and Drug Authority (FDA) permit. Other permits that may be mandatory to have are a fire certificate (permit) and an Environmental Protection Agency (EPA) permit.

> ➢ *What Will Be the Mission, Vision and Values of the Business?*

You have to define the following for your business:

- **Short-term Goals:** They are objectives that can be achieved within a relatively short period of time. It gives you the motivation and confidence to achieve long-term goals. Your short-term goals are the **mission** of your business. An example of a mission or short-term goal can be offering people the best service or product in a certain locality and getting more loyal customers.
- **Long-term Goals:** These give direction, meaning and purpose to the business. They may take several years to achieve. Long-term goals are your business's vision. An example of a vision or long-term goal can be to have the firm's products supplied all over the country and abroad.
- **Values:** They are the internal beliefs, ethics and guiding principles upon which a business bases its objectives and practices. Some of the most common values used by many companies are integrity, honesty, accountability, customer commitment,

respect, innovation, teamwork and passion in a professional setting.

> ### *Where Will Be the Location of My Business?*

The location of your business is the physical place where it will be taking place, and it is dependent on certain factors such as proximity to customers, suppliers, the market, security, taxes, government incentives, rent costs, human resources and operating costs. The location of your business can affect its growth, success, and survival. Take the factors enumerated above into consideration when deciding on the location for your business.

> ### *How Many Branches Am I Going to Establish?*

The number of branches to be established will be dependent on the performance of your business and your customer base. Branches should be sited at a place where the demand for the product or service is high with low operating costs. It should also be sited at a place where you can easily monitor the activities of your staff.

> ### *What Product or Service Will I Be Offering?*

The product or service to be offered will be determined by the recognized problem. The product or service must be designed to help customers solve their problems. It should be a service or product that is scarce in that location and provides value to clients. You should also examine the continual availability of inputs for manufacturing the product and the costs of inputs charged by suppliers.

> ➢ *How Much Capital Is Required to Start My Business?*

Capital is the necessary resource for starting a business. It can be available in various forms, such as money, assets, stocks, or loans. It can be obtained through personal savings or borrowed money from friends, family, or financial institutions. The total capital required depends on the business type, product, office, staff, assets, tools, and operational costs. You need to do a proper estimation before settling on the final figure.

> ➢ *Who Are Going to Be the Customers of My Business?*

Customers are individuals or business entities who buy your products and services. They support your business and drive your revenue. They are the very reason your business exists. Just as the heart is an essential organ in the human body, so are customers for your business.

The way you serve your customers and address their problems is critical to the survival of your business. Remember, I stated that your business must be located where the majority of your customers are. You have to identify them and their challenges even before you decide to start your firm. It is also worth noting that once you stop providing value for money, your customers will soon switch to your competitors.

> ➢ *Who Are the Competitors of the Business I Want to Start?*

Competitors are individuals or business entities that sell similar or substitute products and services to the same target customers. It is very important to know your competitors, what they are offering, their pricing, packaging, customers and their locations. Knowing them will help you develop your market penetration strategies and survive in your business. There are three main classifications of competitors, as described below:

- **Direct Competitors:** They are those who sell the same goods or services in the same market.
- **Indirect Competitors:** They are those who sell different products or services that satisfy the same customer needs.
- **Replacement Competitors:** They are those who provide new products or services, rendering existing ones obsolete.

To stay ahead, you must research customer needs, provide unique products or services, stay updated with technology, and hire skilled workers.

> ➢ *Who Are Going to Be the Suppliers for My Business?*

Suppliers are individuals or business entities that supply products or services to your business. They can be retailers, distributors, manufacturers, or service providers. They play an important role in the supply chain and can assist reduce your operational costs. Before the start of your business, you should have reliable suppliers who can deliver quality products to you on time so that there will not be any shortages.

It is important for you to have more than one supplier because of unforeseen circumstances. You should know their locations, contacts and business terms.

> ### *How Many Workers Am I Going to Employ?*

Workers are the people you employ in your business to assist in delivering quality products or services to your customers. The number of workers you employ is largely dependent on the performance of your business. Many enterprises start with a small number of workers and gradually increase the number as the business flourishes.

You must ensure that you employ people who have the requisite skills and the right attitude for your business. You must not employ people because you want to help them get jobs or because they are your friends or family members. They should have something to offer to help your business grow.

Consider the following qualities when employing workers for your business:

- **Loyalty:** Consider someone who will be committed and devoted to your business.
- **God-fearing:** Consider someone who is earnestly religious.
- **Punctuality:** Consider someone who knows the value of time and will not give excuses for being absent.

- **Proximity:** Consider someone who stays close to the location of your business.
- **Hardworking:** Consider someone who is diligent and not lazy.
- **Integrity:** Consider someone who is ethical and has high moral principles.
- **Secretiveness:** Consider someone who can keep secrets and confidential information.
- **Team Player:** Consider someone who can work with others for business success.
- **Respectfulness:** Consider someone who is courteous and polite and can have reverence for you and your customers.
- **Professionalism:** Consider someone who can adhere to the standards set for the business.
- **Qualification:** Consider someone who has the right credentials to work in your business.
- **Expertise:** Consider someone who has the right experience to work for you.
- **Culture Fit:** Consider someone whose beliefs, values, personality and work styles align with those of your organization.
- **Contentment:** Consider someone who is not envious of others and is satisfied with their own.
- **Trustworthy:** Consider someone you can trust and rely on for the success of your business.

> *What Will Be My Pricing Strategy?*

This is the method you will use to determine the price of your goods or services. Pricing is crucial for businesses, affecting growth and customer retention. Factors to consider in your pricing include mark-up, costs, product life, competitors, value-giving, economic situation, inflation, foreign currency exchange and government regulations.

Now let's consider the various pricing strategies:

- **Cost-Plus Pricing**: This method involves calculating the product's cost and adding a percentage or mark-up to determine the selling price.

- **Competitive Pricing**: Under this method, your price is largely dependent on your competitors' prices. You adjust your competitors' prices for the same products or services to derive your selling price. It is essential to stay aware of market rates and adjust your pricing accordingly.

- **Price Skimming**: Under this method, you initially charge a higher price because the product is new and scarce, but as the market changes and competitors offer substitutes, you gradually begin to lower your price.

- **Value-Based Pricing**: Under this method, the price charge is mostly determined by the value your goods or services provide to your clients. The same goods or services are sold at varying prices in the same locality due to the perceived value the product offers in that place. This is especially popular in premium or luxury markets.

- **Penetration Pricing**: Under this method, you initially charge a lower price for a new product introduced to gain market acceptance, but you gradually increase the price as the market acceptance increases.

- **Psychological or Economy Pricing**: Under this method, you offer goods and services at slightly lower prices to attract price-sensitive customers while increasing the volume of sales. The focus is on cost efficiency and volume sales. This strategy is common in discount stores or budget brands.

> *What Will Be My Marketing Strategy?*

Marketing is crucial for business growth, raising awareness, educating the public and increasing sales. **New entrepreneurs can adopt the below strategies to effectively promote their products.**

- **Free Sample:** You can share samples of your products with people to create awareness and encourage patronage for your business.

- **Flyers, Brochures and Complementary Cards:** You can ask someone to design flyers, brochures and complimentary cards for sharing with different people and at various vantage points.

- **In-Person Marketing:** You can do one-on-one marketing for your new product or business.

- **Social Media Handles:** You have to leverage your social media handles to create awareness about your products and business.
- **Sales Outlets:** You can create sales outlets in various areas to serve the people in that locality and boost your sales and customer base.
- **Distribution to Various Shops and Stores:** You can also make arrangements with supermarkets, shops and stores to display and sell some of your products.
- **Head Potters Sales:** You can also give some of your products to individuals to sell at various functions, marketplaces, etc.

> ➤ *What Bookkeeping and Accounting Software Is Required for My Business?*

Bookkeeping is very important for your business, as it will help you ascertain the performance and financial position of your business. The tax authorities will also demand your financial records to determine taxes to be paid to the government.

To aid in this, you may require simple bookkeeping software such as QuickBooks or Tally when the business starts flourishing. However, you may use a spreadsheet (Microsoft Excel) to keep track of your income and expenditures until you acquire the software. Remember, you may require the services of an accounting officer if you lack knowledge of the use of accounting software.

➢ *What Are the Assets Required for My Business?*

You need assets to be able to run your business and generate income. Focus on assets that are only needed, and with time, you can add on when needed. The assets to acquire depend on your type of business and the service or product you are offering. Do not invest in assets that are not urgently needed because you will incur repairs and maintenance costs on them. Also, the value of the assets depreciates with time. Assets can be **tangible (physical) or intangible (financial).** Chapter 4 has the details of all the assets you need to know. Take time to read about them.

➢ *What Taxes Will Be Required by My Business to Pay?*

As a citizen, you may be required to pay taxes to your government in accordance with the tax laws of your country. The taxes to be paid depend on the form of your business.

Basically, we can talk of three forms of business, as per below:

- **Sole Proprietorship:** This form of business is organized and run by one person. Sole proprietorship is also **called a one-man business.** The owner bears all the risks of the business and enjoys the profit of the business alone.

   The separate legal entity concept does not apply to this form of business as the owner is not separated from the business. Most countries add the profit made from this business to all other income generated by the owner within a period and tax it according to **pay-as-you-earn (PAYE) rates.** Under this form of business, you may also be required to pay **value-added tax (VAT)** if you meet a threshold specified by the VAT laws. Lastly, your business may be required to pay **withholding taxes and PAYE** for people employed in your business.

- **Partnership:** It is a form of business where there is an arrangement by two or more people to contribute resources to run and manage a business with the aim of sharing the profit that will be made from the business. Profit sharing is made in accordance with the ratio enshrined in what we call a partnership deed or agreement.

  In some countries, profits shared by the individual partners are usually added to their other income and taxed according to the country's **pay-as-you-earn (PAYE) rates.** Under this form of business, the partnership firm may also be required to pay **value-added tax (VAT)** if it meets a threshold specified by the VAT laws. Lastly, the partnership firm may be required to pay **withholding taxes** and **PAYE** for people employed in the business.

- **Limited Liability Company:** This is the most complex form of business, and its owners' liability in the company is limited to the amount of money invested in the business. This means that, in the event of the liquidation or collapse of the company, the owners' investment that can be lost is the amount invested in the business. Its owners are called shareholders.

The separate legal entity concept applies to this form of business as the owners and management of the company are separated from the company itself. The company has its own rights and obligations. It can sue and be sued. Some of the taxes paid by this form of business are **company income tax (CIT), withholding taxes, PAYE, VAT, customs duties, levies, penalties, interest,** etc.

> ➤ *What Education Do I Need to Be Successful in My Business?*

You must always research and learn more about new technology, trends, products and assets if you want to stay ahead of your competitors and offer the best quality product or service to your customers. You must attend seminars and trainings on leadership and how to run a successful business in the face of challenges. You can also partner with top brands for mutual benefits. Continuous learning is a requirement for entrepreneurs.

Some of the recommended trainings for entrepreneurs are as follows:
- Financial Analysis for Decision-Making
- Risk Management
- Fundraising and Financing
- Leadership
- Introduction to Microsoft Applications
- Brand Positioning

- Staff Management
- Taxation

Congratulations if you have been able to provide the answers to the above seventeen **(17)** questions. I strongly believe they will be beneficial in guiding you to establish your own business. If you require further assistance, please seek the advice of an expert.

❖ *Risks Faced by Entrepreneurs*

Risk is defined as an unknown event or series of events that have an impact on achieving your goals, as measured by the probability of a perceived threat or opportunity occurring and the magnitude of its effects on your goals.

Every business comes with risks, and as a result, you will be exposed to some risks as a new entrepreneur.

Now let's look at some of the risks you will face as an entrepreneur:

✓ *Financial Risk*

Seed capital, sourced from banks, friends, family, or personal savings, is crucial for entrepreneurs to start their businesses. However, the risk of losing all invested capital is high. Entrepreneurs should be able to take measures to mitigate this risk.

✓ *Market Risk*

There is the market entry risk that is usually faced by new entrepreneurs, as the existing ones may collude against the new ones through price reductions and other market strategies.

✓ *Competitive Risks*

New entrepreneurs always face stiff competition from their existing firms as they come up with counter-attack strategies to collapse the new business. The competitors sometimes introduce similar products at affordable prices just to steal customers and the market.

✓ *Technology Risk*

New technologies are constantly emerging, necessitating significant investment in new systems and processes for competitiveness. This technological investment requires huge capital, which could be a problem for entrepreneurs.

✓ *Reputational Risks*

A new business reputation is crucial, as first impressions count, especially when customers have high expectations. If a new firm disappoints customers in the initial stages, it may never gain traction, negatively impacting the new business. Entrepreneurs must put effective market penetration strategies in place before launching their products or services.

❖ *Risk Management Strategies for Entrepreneurs*

Risk management is a systematic approach to identifying, assessing and addressing potential threats or uncertainties that may impact an organization.

Now, let's look at some of the risk management strategies.

- **Identifying Potential Risks:** Perform a comprehensive risk analysis across all business areas, identifying competitive, market, financial, technological, and reputational risks and developing contingency plans for high-impact risks.

- **Risk Analysis:** Before making any decisions, consider the risks inherent in a specific business or investment. Assess risks in terms of probability and effect. This enables you to make informed decisions.

- **Insurance:** Invest in suitable insurance policies, such as asset-all-risks, general liability and workers' compensation insurance, to safeguard your business from unforeseen events.

- **Business Plan:** Develop a comprehensive business plan that outlines risk management techniques, risk tolerance levels and mitigation actions for specific risks.

- **Diversification:** Diversify your company's activities by looking into new markets, products, or services to mitigate the risks associated with relying on a single revenue source.

- **Risk Anticipation:** Staying informed about industry trends, regulatory changes, and economic shifts helps anticipate potential risks and adapt business strategies accordingly.

❖ *Some Common Traits or Qualities of Entrepreneurs*

- **Risk-taker:** Most areas of business revolve around taking risks and experimenting. You may succeed or fail. To accomplish your goals, you must be willing to take risks.
- **Rule Breaker:** You should be able to challenge the status quo and establish new ones.
- **Flexible:** You should be able to adjust to changing situations.
- **Visionary:** You should know where you want to take your business in the future. You must set long-term business objectives.
- **Leader:** You should be an effective leader who leads by example. To be a good leader, you must be disciplined and have high moral standards.
- **Goal-setter:** You should be able to set specified, measurable, achievable, realistic and time-bound goals (SMART).
- **Responsible:** You should accept responsibility for the consequences of your actions and decisions.
- **Decision-maker:** You should be able to stand your ground and make hard decisions when required.
- **Problem Solver:** You should have problem-solving abilities because your workers will look to you as a last resort.
- **Planner:** You must be able to plan and think ahead. Consider the possibilities beyond the present.
- **Organizer:** You should be capable of organizing your company's activities and human resources.

- **Competitor:** You should not be afraid to compete with others for the same thing you seek.
- **Team Builder:** You should be able to build up your team during times of disagreement and conflict.
- **Innovative:** You must be able to identify new opportunities and implement new company practices.
- **Knowledgeable:** You should have an extensive understanding of the industry to which you belong. Knowledge is critical for success and problem-solving.

❖ *Skills Required by Entrepreneurs*
- Customer service, sales and marketing
- Communication and negotiation skills
- Leadership
- Delegation and time management
- Networking
- Financial management
- Human resource management
- Information Technology (IT)

In summary, the relationship between wealth and entrepreneurship is multifaceted. Entrepreneurs contribute to the overall accumulation of wealth in society. By creating successful businesses, they generate value and prosperity.

Chapter 12: Spiritual Ways for Activating Wealth

It is important to understand that the spiritual always controls the physical, and likewise, there are spiritual things that can be done to activate physical wealth. Hard work is good, but that is not the only thing that can make you wealthy, and this can easily be substantiated by the saying of many people that they work **"like an elephant but get paid like an ant."** Even at the workplace, the people who do the hard work are the junior staff, yet they receive the minimum pay.

It is also an undeniable fact that most people who normally engage in skilled work, such as masons, carpenters, welders, drivers, mechanics, and plant and machinery operators, earn a lower daily minimum wage than those who work in the office. The jobs of the above-mentioned people are riskier and more life-threatening than those in the office, yet most of them are paid less.

We often hear that **"education is the key to success,"** with which I agree to some extent. However, we all need to understand that education is not the only thing that makes people successful and wealthy. In fact, the wealthiest people in this world are not educators or professors. Most of them either dropped out of school or did not continue their education after their first degree and yet, because of their wealth and success, they have the most prestigious honorary doctorate degrees conferred on them.

I am not in any way trying to despise or undermine the importance of education. All I am trying to do is to make you understand that beyond hard work and education, there are other equally important things that can be done to activate and sustain wealth or success in this world. Please be open-minded and learn and practise what works best for you.

Finally, my advice to you is to seek education, work hard and apply the practical ways I am about to discuss, and everything will be fine for you.

Now let's look at some of the practical spiritual ways that have helped some people become wealthy and successful:

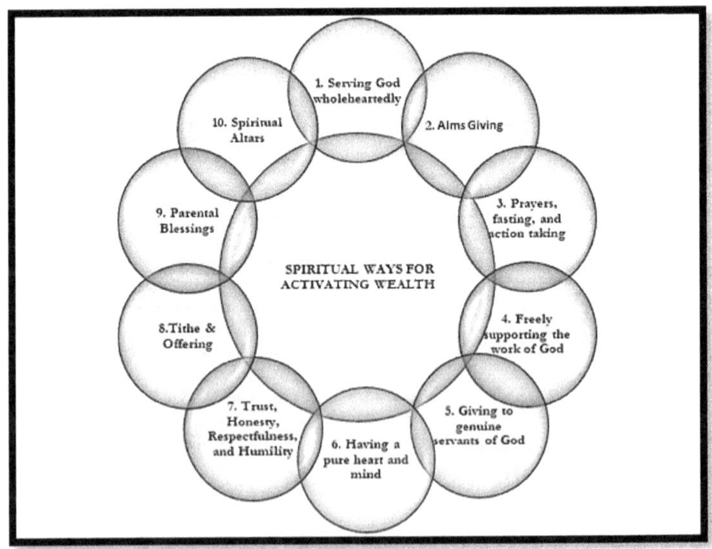

Figure 12.1

➢ *Serving God Wholeheartedly*

It is important for you to know that everybody in this world serves something and that there is no middle ground. There is someone who created the world we live in and owns everything in it, including you. If you say you are worshipping God almighty, then you have to worship Him wholeheartedly. You need to be obedient to Him and trust Him. The God you serve is your spiritual father, who gives you everything. He has the power to bless and make you wealthy through all the mediums for generating money, as discussed in **Chapter 5**.

Consider the following verses, which project God Almighty as the giver of wealth:

- ***Deuteronomy 8:18*** *– And you shall remember the Lord your God, for it is He who gives you power to get wealth, that He may establish His covenant which He swore to your fathers, as it is this day.*

- ***Philippians 4:19*** *– And my God shall supply all your need according to His riches in glory by Christ Jesus.*

- ***1 Chronicles 29:12*** *– Wealth and honor come from you; you are the ruler of all things. In your hands are strength and power to exalt and give strength to all.*

- ***Deuteronomy 2:7*** *– "For the Lord your God has blessed you in all the work of your hand. He knows you are trudging through this great wilderness. These forty years the Lord your God has been with you; you have lacked nothing."*

➢ *Alms Giving*

This is about giving part of your resources, such as money, clothes, food and drinks, assets, and others, to the destitute, orphans, widows and the vulnerable in our society. There is a popular saying that **"givers never lack,"** which emphasizes the importance of giving. Anytime you give, you activate the numerous blessing and wealth doors that have been shut in your life. You can be sure that all the people you give to will be praying for more blessings in your life so that you can always remember them. Do not be forced to give, but instead, give willingly and from a good heart. For a better activation, always add this to your yearly budget, and you will never regret it.

Consider the following verses, which endorse alms-giving:

- *Proverbs 19:17 (Bible) – He who has pity on the poor lends to the Lord, And He will pay back what he has given.*
- *Luke 6:38 (Bible) – Give, and it will be given to you: good measure, pressed down, shaken together, and running over will be put into your bosom. For with the same measure that you use, it will be measured back to you.*
- *Colossians 3:23(Bible) – "Whatever you do, work at it with all your heart, as working for the Lord, not for human masters."*
- *Proverbs 28:27 (Bible) – He who gives to the poor will not lack, but he who hides his eyes will have many curses.*

- *2 Corinthians 9:7 (Bible)* – *So let each one give as he purposes in his heart, not grudgingly or of necessity; for God loves a cheerful giver.*

- *Ephesians 4:28 (Bible)* – *Let him who stole steal no longer, but rather let him labor, working with his hands what is good, that he may have something to give him who has need.*

- *Surah Al-Baqarah 2:236(Qur'an)* – *But give them [a gift of] compensation – the wealthy according to his capability and the poor according to his capability – a provision according to what is acceptable, a duty upon the doers of good.*

- *Surah Ali 'Imran3:92 (Qur'an)* – *By no means shall you attain righteousness unless you give freely of that which you love, and whatever you give, Allah knows it well.*

> *Prayers, Fasting and Action Taking*

Prayer is simply communication between you and your God. Just as I have already mentioned, God is your spiritual father, and you are expected to communicate with Him on every issue that borders you. The truth is, He is always prepared to listen to you, but the question is: Are you ready to talk to Him? And when He talks, do you hear His voice? Many people take decisions or steps and do things without finding out from their God if what they want to do will end well or not. Unfortunately, they blame God if it backfires. Fasting is simply denying yourself worldly pleasures for a variety of reasons, including building your spiritual capacity. It helps strengthen our relationship with God.

Please note that taking the necessary actions after fasting and praying to your God is very important to unlocking the wealth or blessings you seek. Many people fast and pray, but unfortunately, they ignore the action part. This explains why many prayer warriors and Christians still remain poor. For instance, if you fast and pray for a job and God directs you to send your CV to a certain company and you refuse to take action, do you think you will get the job? Likewise, faith without action is dead. With **fervent prayer, fasting and other necessary actions**, you can unlock certain dimensions of wealth. **Take action now!**

Check out the verse below:

- ***Surah Maryam Ayat 19:31(Qur'an)*** *– And He has made me blessed wherever I am and has enjoined upon me Prayer and Zakah as long as I remain alive.*

➢ *Freely Supporting the Work of God*

Don't be like people who always say that they worship God in their hearts and, as a result, will never support any work of God. Worshipping God is personal, but when you are in a position to support a worthy cause, please do so, as your **kind deeds will pursue you**. One of the most effective ways of activating wealth and blessings is to personally identify things that are needed by God's church and buy them without disclosing your identity. Anytime you buy such things, pray over them with your heart's desires and send someone to deliver them to the church. You will be amazed by the outcome. Moreover, what will be your justification for God to save you in times of adversity if you don't do something for him now?

Consider the following verses for your enlightenment:

- ***2 Corinthians 9:7*** *– So let each one give as he purposes in his heart, not grudgingly or of necessity; for God loves a cheerful giver.*
- ***Ecclesiastes 11:1*** *– Cast your bread upon the waters, for you will find it after many days.*
- ***Ephesians 2:10*** *– "For we are His workmanship, created in Christ Jesus for good works, which God prepared beforehand so that we would walk in them."*

➢ *Giving to Genuine Servants of God*

Apart from God, who is your spiritual father, there are servants of God and people that God has positioned in your life to be your helpers and guardians. It is important to factor these people into your budget and surprise them from time to time. Doing this will provide a spiritual covering or protection for you. God will open doors of wealth and blessings for you so you can also support His servants. Keep and value the relationship you have with them, and they will keep praying for you. Many people forget the pillars that they lean on when things go well. Do not be part of them, as it can be dangerous. Wealthy and successful people have spiritual people who support them with prayers and directions. Don't be like **"a chick without a hen."** You will be vulnerable.

Consider the following verses for your enlightenment:

- *Matthew 10:41 – He who receives a prophet in the name of a prophet shall receive a prophet's reward. And he who receives a righteous man in the name of a righteous man shall receive a righteous man's reward.*

- *2 Chronicles 20:20 – So they rose early in the morning and went out into the Wilderness of Tekoa; and as they went out, Jehoshaphat stood and said, "Hear me, O Judah and you inhabitants of Jerusalem, Believe in the Lord your God, and you shall be established; believe His prophets, and you shall prosper."*

- *Amos 3:7 – "Surely the Lord God will do nothing, but he revealeth his secret unto his servants the prophets."*

➢ *Having a Pure Heart and Mind*

It is important for you to develop a pure heart and a pure mind, which is a state of inner purity. Do not scheme evil against people, as what you wish for them will automatically become your portion someday. Karma is real and works right here in our world. Don't rejoice over people's predicaments. Remember, vengeance is from God, so try to forgive often, as unforgiveness blocks blessings and doors from opening. The end of the wicked is always terrible. You will see positive results as you adhere to the above principles.

Consider the following verses for your enlightenment:

- *Matthew 7:12* –*"In everything, therefore, treat people the same way you want them to treat you, for this is the Law and the Prophets."*
- *Luke 6:31* – *"Treat others the same way you want them to treat you."*
- *Matthew 5:8* – *"Blessed are the pure in heart, For they shall see God."*
- *Proverbs 12:5* – *"The thoughts of the righteous are right, but the counsels of the wicked are deceitful."*

➢ ***Trust, Honesty, Respectfulness and Humility***

It will be difficult to access certain dimensions of wealth if you lack humility, honesty, respect and trust. You can be very talented, intelligent, or hardworking and still be poor if you don't have the above qualities. People will love to work with you and entrust things to you only if you possess these qualities. People have lost great opportunities and fortunes because of these traits. No matter the situation, please don't compromise on these traits, as there are hidden treasures in them.

➢ ***Tithe and Offering***

Tithing is all about giving **10%** of every income you earn or receive to support the work of God **(church activities)**. Many tithers have given several incredible testimonies of the blessings they have received since they started tithing. This 10% is not part of the alms you give or other support you give to your church. With tithe, you are just acknowledging that everything you have belongs to God, and you are just a steward of them. You give **10% to God**, and you **retain 90% for yourself**. Offerings are freewill, and the amount or percentage to give is solely determined by you.

Consider the following verses for your enlightenment:

- *Leviticus 27:30 – And all the tithe of the land, whether of the seed of the land or of the fruit of the tree, is the Lord's. It is holy to the Lord.*

- *Hebrews 7:1-2 – For this Melchizedek, king of Salem, priest of the Most High God, met Abraham returning from the slaughter of the kings and blessed him, and to him Abraham apportioned a tenth part of everything.*

- *Malachi 3:10 – "Bring all the tithes into the storehouse, That there may be food in My house, And try Me now in this," says the Lord of hosts, "If I will not open for you the windows of heaven And pour out for you such blessing, that there will not be room enough to receive it."*

➤ *Parental Blessings*

The act of bestowing God's blessings on one's children is known as a parental blessing. Your parents have the opportunity to speak words of love, encouragement and blessing over you, which can have a lasting impact on your life. Parental blessings are powerful declarations of love, protection and support that can make you feel encouraged, valued and inspired.

Throughout history, parental blessings have been valued. It originated with the patriarchs and is considered a sacred rite. You should seek blessings from your parents or guardians, as it can open doors to unimaginable opportunities for you. These blessings are extremely meaningful, going beyond mere words to touch the hearts and souls of the people who receive them. You can read **Genesis 49:1–27** when Jacob blessed his twelve sons and outlined what was ahead of them.

One blessing that parents typically give while blessing their children is from *Numbers 6:24-26:*
24 – "The Lord bless you and keep you."
25 – "The Lord let his face shine on you and be gracious to you."
26 – "The Lord looks upon you kindly and gives you peace."

➢ *Spiritual Altars*

Altars have great spiritual significance in the Bible, as they are associated with numerous aspects of faith, worship and divine encounters. In the Bible, altars were used to facilitate communication between God and mankind. They symbolized sacrifice, thanksgiving, divine encounters and reminders of God's promises. People used these altars to fully consecrate themselves to the Lord, displaying their faith and devotion.

The altar transcended the physical realm and represented humanity's spiritual link with God. Our forefathers utilized altars as receptacles for concrete demonstrations of their faith, presenting sacrifices as a sign of their dedication and love for their God.

Similarly, many people today have erected altars in their houses where they usually meet their God. This is a spiritual dwelling place that allows them to focus on their worship and communication with God. It is devoid of noise and impurity. These people have shared numerous testimonies regarding the blessings received since they made the altar in their houses. You can give it a try if you believe in it.

Chapter 13|
Places to Save and Invest

Many people ask, "Where can we save and invest our funds?" Due to the high number of fraud and scam incidents reported each year, numerous people are now afraid of and discouraged from saving and investing their funds. It is also worth noting that there are various Ponzi schemes in the system that claim to offer high interest rates or returns on investments.

Unfortunately, many people have become victims of these Ponzi schemes. Money is difficult to come by these days, so you must conduct due diligence on the place where you intend to save and invest. I have extensively discussed how to gather credible information for decision-making regarding saving and investing in **Chapter 9 (Wealth and Information)**.

Please take your time and read the different sources of investment or financial information, as they will be useful to you.

Let me also take this opportunity to admonish you that it is always better to invest for smaller returns than to lose everything you have to unregulated schemes that seek to dupe you and cannot also be traced in times of danger. Creating or building wealth is a gradual process that requires patience and discipline. Many people were doing so well for themselves but lost everything they had worked so hard for due to their greed and thirst for quick wealth, power and fame.

How can you invest in Ponzi schemes that promise **10% to 20%** monthly returns while registered commercial banks and investment companies provide just **3% to 5%**? This should be a **red flag** for you unless you are inexperienced in financial issues. After reading this book, I expect you to make better decisions about financial investments and savings.

Finally, keep in mind that the best place to save or invest is heavily influenced by your savings or investment objectives, the amount of due diligence performed, the expected returns, and a variety of other considerations.

Let's have a look at the different places you might save or invest your available funds.

NO.	10 PLACES TO SAVE AND INVEST
1	Registered and licensed commercial banks
2	Investment banks or companies
3	Credit union
4	Insurance companies
5	Limited Liability Company
6	Real Estate Investment Trusts (REITs)
7	Pension fund trustees or companies
8	Brokerage firms
9	Rural and Community Banks
10	Digital or online investment platforms

Figure 13.1

> ➤ *Registered and Licensed Commercial Banks*

These are the banks registered by the government authority responsible for registering businesses and also licensed by the central bank of the country in which they operate. Mostly, these commercial banks are issued operating licenses only if they meet the minimum capital requirements and other conditions outlined by the central bank. These commercial banks can only carry out activities for which they have been licensed. Any infractions on their part attract severe sanctions by the central bank.

You can transact the following with them:

- **Fixed Deposit:** You can purchase fixed deposits, which are provided by commercial banks and usually have higher interest rates than a normal savings account.

- **Savings Account:** This is a type of bank account that allows you to save while earning interest. It usually has a limited monthly withdrawal limit. You can open a savings account with a licensed bank.

- **Treasury Bills:** Treasury bills are a form of borrowing by a national government for a period of time, usually up to one year, on which interest is paid at the end of the borrowing period. Treasury bills are short-term debt instruments (securities) issued by the governments of many nations with a maturity of less than one year. **They commonly have maturities of 91 days, 182 days and 364 days.** You can purchase treasury bills through a registered and licensed bank.

- **Bonds:** Bonds are investment securities in which an investor lends money to a corporation or government for a specified length of time in exchange for a steady stream of payments (**also known as interest payments or coupons**). At the end of the bond's tenure or lifetime, the lender receives **100 percent of the bond's face value**. You can purchase government bonds through licensed commercial banks.

- **Bancassurance:** It is an agreement between a bank and an insurance firm in which the bank sells insurance to its customers. The bank and the insurance firm share the commissions earned. You can buy investment plans offered by insurance providers through banks.

- **Forex Account:** You can open a foreign-denominated account with commercial banks in USD, Euro, or Pounds to take advantage of foreign currency fluctuations.

- **Purchase Precious Minerals:** You can invest in other tangible assets, such as minerals, through commercial banks. To purchase gold, inquire about the bank's physical gold products, compare their pricing to market and spot prices, select your gold option and obtain the necessary certifications. Gold can be purchased in the form of coins, bars, ingots and wafers.

- **Other Investment Products:** You can also subscribe to bank-sold investment products like a home-save, a house plan, or a wealth plan. The majority of these products are designed to help you save money for a new home or land. These investment products, or accounts, attract interest.

➢ ***Investment Banks or Companies***

Unlike commercial banks, which only accept deposits and provide loans to customers, investment companies trade in capital market securities such as mutual funds, stocks, bonds, derivatives, futures and options. They are licensed and regulated by the Securities and Exchange Commission (SEC). A capital market is a financial market where long-term debt or equity-backed securities are purchased and sold, as opposed to a money market, which purchases and sells short-term debt. The capital market is made up of organized security exchanges and over-the-counter markets. Physical trading arrangements take place on organized security exchanges. Trading arrangements outside of organized security exchanges take place in over-the-counter markets. You can purchase any of the above-mentioned products from licensed investment banks or companies in your country. Kindly visit the Security and Exchange Commission (SEC) website for a published list of good-standing investment companies.

➢ ***Credit Unions***

They are financial institutions mostly owned by their registered members and provide various products and services. They are mostly unregulated by national central banks. They are typically licensed and governed by credit union bodies in various nations. They are non-profit organizations whose primary goal is to deliver high-quality services to their members, not to maximize profits. To use the union's products or services, you must first register to become a member. They typically provide services similar to those of a bank. You can save and invest with them if you join the union. Credit unions typically provide higher interest rates on savings and lower interest rates on loans.

➢ *Insurance Companies*

Insurance companies provide indemnity or cover against financial losses due to theft, natural occurrences, accidents and other unforeseen events. Policyholders pay premiums for the insurance coverage they receive and get indemnified by the insurance company whenever there is an occurrence. For example, you might buy motor comprehensive insurance to protect your life, your car, and a third party whenever there is an accident. Some insurance companies have investment products such as education and life insurance. You can buy some of these investment products.

➢ *Limited Liability Company*

This is a registered company, and its owners' liability in the company is limited to the amount of money invested in the business. They can offer a direct purchase option to investors for capital. They also issue bonds to raise funds from individual and corporate investors. You can invest in these shares and bonds whenever the opportunity arises.

➢ *Real Estate Investment Trusts (REITs)*

REITs allow you to invest in real estate without directly owning property. They generate income from rent and property appreciation.

➢ *Pension Fund Trustees or Companies*

These are pension companies that have various pension plans or schemes and allow individuals to save and invest their funds with them for a better future retirement. They are usually licensed and regulated by various nations' pension regulatory authorities or administrations. The investment plans are available for company employees as well as individuals. Their pension schemes have tax advantages, which help you save for retirement. Contributions may be tax-deductible or tax-free, depending on the period for which you contribute.

➢ *Brokerage Firms*

These are firms that help broker transactions. They serve as an intermediary between those who want to buy and those who want to sell securities such as stocks, mutual funds and bonds. You can only buy securities when others are selling theirs. Having an investment account with a brokerage firm can help facilitate trading transactions. They often charge fees or commissions for their services.

➢ *Rural and Community Banks*

These are banks that provide banking services to people living in remote or rural areas. They serve a smaller number of customers than commercial banks. They are also licensed and regulated by the central banks of various countries. They also offer savings and investment products to their customers.

> ➢ *Digital or Online Investment Platforms*

These are online platforms that offer people the opportunity to make online investments for a higher return. As it stands now, most of these online platforms are difficult for the authorities or administrations of various countries to regulate. You have to be extremely careful when investing online. A lot of people have been duped by online fraudsters who launched investment products. You are advised to consult investment consultants before investing online.

> ✓ *Conclusion*

Understanding where you may save and invest is critical for making sound financial decisions. You can determine the finest solutions for your needs and tastes by researching the various organizations' products. Whether you are saving for a rainy day, investing for the future, or borrowing money for a large purchase, financial institutions or companies can help you reach your financial goals. Remember that each investment opportunity has unique risk-reward trade-offs. Prior to making a selection, consider your financial situation, ambitions and risk tolerance. Diversifying your investments might also improve overall portfolio stability. Happy saving and investing!

Chapter 14|
Wealth Preservation for Future Generation

Wealth preservation entails measures to protect present wealth from erosion or loss and provide asset value protection, risk reduction and long-term financial security for individuals and future generations. It also involves protecting portfolios from loss and maintaining purchasing power over time. Investing in commodities, real estate, or inflation-protected securities ensures growth and maintains assets' value.

It is important for you to put adequate measures in place to secure all your wealth. As I previously stated, resources are scarce, and if you are fortunate enough to have them, the best thing you can do is to protect them for your immediate family and future generations.

It is crucial for you to understand that the value of your wealth can be depleted owing to variables such as inflation, risk, recession and foreign currency fluctuations, among others. As a result, appropriate safeguards must be put in place to protect your wealth.

Remember, the goal is to always increase your wealth so that you can reach the abundance level of wealth where money will never be a problem for you and you can make a significant impact in the lives of others and the entire world. It will be very senseless for you to work and amass so much wealth without any proper protection. Draft a will or advance medical directive to ensure your wishes are honored in the event of death. A durable power of attorney for healthcare is also necessary for decision-making in non-advanced medical situations.

One of the major problems you will face if you become abundantly rich is finding the right person to be your successor to ensure that your financial or wealth legacy can be extended to the next generation. This problem of choosing the right successor can be resolved if you start early by introducing your children to the concept of finance or wealth.

What we often see about the wealthy is that they introduce their children early to their businesses and train them about finances and wealth-making. Some even give some key roles in their companies to their children. All these are meant to train, educate and prepare them for smooth succession.

Similarly, you can also begin to educate and train your children about business, finances, budgeting, savings and investments. You do not need to have more wealth before you begin to train them. You can start by opening a kid's savings account for them at a bank. This will give them banking experience and the motivation to study hard and get involved in your business. Remember, charity begins at home.

Finally, it is crucial to mention that your legacy cannot be extended to future generations unless handed over to the right person. That is why it is more important to prepare your successors early and introduce them to all your businesses and the wealth you have.

I must say that the person will take quite a while to settle and grasp everything you want them to know. You need to consider the character, maturity level, interest of the successors in what you want to hand over to them, and willingness to work hard so that your wealth will not be depleted.

Now let's look at some of the measures that can preserve your wealth for future generations:

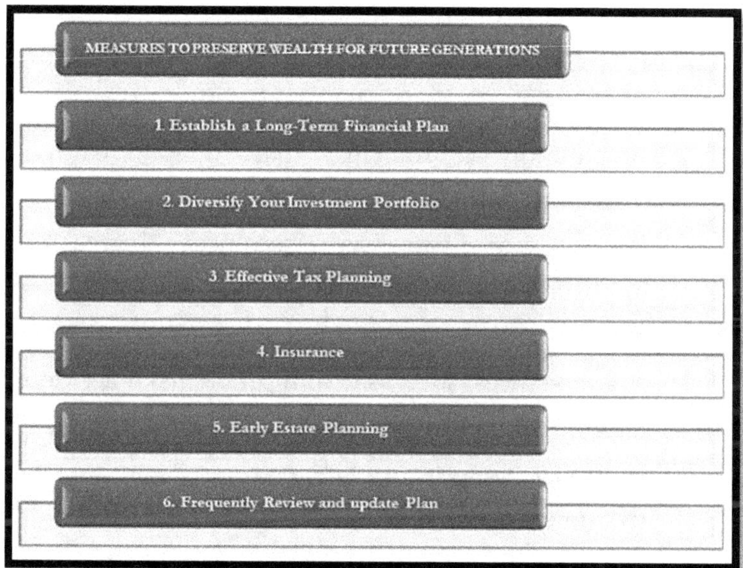

Figure 14.1

- **Establish a Long-Term Financial Plan**: Establish specific financial objectives, set a budget and review your overall financial plan on a regular basis. Life may be unpredictable, but having a firm foundation allows you to plan for unforeseen needs without depleting your long-term assets.

- **Diversify Your Investment Portfolio**: A well-balanced investment portfolio can help you weather market volatility and reduce risk, especially if you have a fixed income. Diversification across asset classes can also help you maintain stability and protect your investment. To manage risks, diversify your portfolio across asset classes like stocks, bonds, and real estate and use hedging strategies like putting options or shorting stocks.

- **Effective Tax Planning**: Use tax-advantaged accounts to reduce your tax bills. Proper tax preparation guarantees that your wealth is preserved and effectively handled.

- **Insurance:** Insurance becomes increasingly important for risk management as you become older. It protects against unanticipated circumstances, such as health problems or accidents. Explore alternatives such as life insurance, health insurance, long-term care insurance, and asset-all-risk insurance.

- **Early Estate Planning**: Ensure a smooth transition of wealth to future generations. Estate planning entails drafting wills, trusts and other legal papers to disperse assets as you intend. Start early to avoid future issues.

- **Frequently Review and Update Plan**: Since goals vary over time, it is important to review and update your financial plan on a regular basis. Be adaptable and prepared to pivot as necessary. Remember that money is a tool for achieving your life goals, such as travelling, retiring, or supporting loved ones.

Remember, building and preserving wealth requires careful planning, execution and disciplined measures to protect assets from market volatility, achieve long-term growth and focus on long-term goals. Wealth preservation is a continuous effort that requires attention, vision and adaptability. By applying these tactics, you can ensure a prosperous financial future for yourself and your family.

Chapter 15|
Final Thoughts on Wealth Creation

Let me take this opportunity to congratulate you if you have been able to read this great masterpiece. I firmly believe that you have been greatly impacted by the content of this book, just as I have also been affected by the truth presented. I must say that taking time out of my busy schedule to write this book was never easy; however, it has been a great, insightful and refreshing moment for me. Welcome to a different level of life where those who know the secrets to wealth rule over those who do not.

You might have discovered by now that wealth creation is not by magic; instead, it is a purposeful and intentional attempt to learn and understand all the pros and cons of wealth and finances. It will be meaningless for you to have read this book without making a conscious effort to make the necessary changes to your finances and attitude. So please start making the changes now.

Also, you might have learned from this book that even before you begin your wealth creation journey, you should be able to outline your own wealth creation objectives, just as Thomas Carlyle said: *"A man without a goal is like a ship without a rudder tossed by the tempestuous waves. Without a compass to guide him, he drifts aimlessly, caught between the vast expanse of sky and water. The wind whispers secrets, but he cannot decipher their meaning. His sails flap uselessly, seeking purpose in the empty horizon."* In essence, if you lack direction, it will be difficult for you to achieve anything, including wealth.

This book contains a chapter dedicated to highlighting the importance of financial literacy. Change is constant in this world. To stay updated at all times, you must continually read and listen to financial and investment news. You must be informed of any changes or new developments in investment or financial matters. Anything that has the potential to affect your wealth should be a major concern for you. Please make time to attend investment and finance seminars and conferences.

I cannot go without mentioning the most important components of wealth. Assets, liabilities, income and expenditure are all key components of wealth creation. The way you create and use them has a direct impact on your overall wealth. That is why I spent so much time discussing them in depth. You should be conversant with the various investment vehicles, such as stocks, bonds, mutual funds and T-Bills. The different types of liabilities, income and expenditures were also thoroughly discussed for your study.

Mindset is crucial in everything we do as humans; therefore, maintain a good mindset and believe in yourself that you can succeed no matter what life throws at you. There will be moments when things are smooth and times when they are not. They are all part of life's journey. Do not be disheartened by naysayers; instead, be driven by the success of others, learn from successful investors and proceed at your own pace.

Remember that creating wealth is a gradual process that involves patience, perseverance, hard work and dedication to your goals. The affluent cry and make mistakes, so it is natural for you to cry and make mistakes on your journey.

In addition, you need to note the elements of balanced wealth, which include time, money, talents, holistic well-being, wisdom and networks or relationships. Though it is important to pursue wealth, you must not pursue it at the expense of other equally important aspects of your life.

You must have time for yourself and your family or loved ones. You must not ignore your God-given talents and wisdom. In fact, these talents and wisdom can even enable you to make more wealth. **Let your health be a priority for you, as a dead man does not enjoy wealth,** and have a healthy relationship with your acquaintances, as you are not an island.

Lastly, you have to understand that the spiritual controls the physical, and as enshrined in this book, there are spiritual ways of activating wealth. Follow the spiritual ways enumerated, and you will definitely be amazed by the outcome. The only thing that is unavoidable is death. **Prepare your successors early and make a will before any unanticipated event.** I know you are not a fool to work so hard for the wrong people to enjoy your legacy. Therefore, put your house in order now that you have strength.

Please, if this book has been helpful to you, kindly recommend it to your friends and loved ones so that they can also be enlightened.

Appendix:
Wealth and Finance Quotes

1. *"The best preparation for tomorrow is doing your best today." — H. Jackson Brown Jr*

2. *"The rich invest their money and spend what is left; the poor spend their money and invest what is left." — Jim Rohn*

3. *"Wealth is not about having a lot of money; it's about having a lot of options." — Chris Rock*

4. *"The person who doesn't know where his next dollar is coming from usually doesn't know where his last dollar went." — Frank A. Clark*

5. *"Wealth is the slave of a wise man and the master of a fool." — Seneca*

6. *"Wealth is the product of man's capacity to think." — Ayn Rand*

7. *"He who buys what he does not need will someday need what he cannot buy." — Unknown*

8. *"It's easy to be rich when you don't need anything." — Unknown*

9. *"The only way to permanently change the temperature in the room is to reset the thermostat. In the same way, the only way to change your level of financial success 'permanently' is to reset your financial thermostat." — T. Harv Eker*

10. *"If you want to be rich, think of yourself as rich." — Unknown*

11. *"Wealth is the ability to say 'yes' to the things you want and 'no' to the things you don't want." — Unknown*

12. *"The more you learn, the more you earn." — Warren Buffett*

13. *"Money is only a tool. It will take you wherever you wish, but it will not replace you as the driver." — Ayn Rand*

14. *"The real measure of your wealth is how much you'd be worth if you lost all your money." — Unknown*

15. *"Wealth is not an absolute. It's relative to desire. Every time we yearn for something we can't afford, we grow poorer, whatever our resources. And every time we feel satisfied with what we have, we can be counted as rich, however little we may actually possess." — Alain de Botton*

16. *"Wealth is not his that has it, but his that enjoys it." — Benjamin Franklin*

17. *"Don't tell me where your priorities are. Show me where you spend your money and I'll tell you what they are." — James W. Frick*

18. *"The key to making money is to stay invested." — Suze Orman*

19. *"The secret of getting ahead is getting started." — Mark Twain*

20. *"It's not about ideas. It's about making ideas happen." — Scott Belsky*

21. *"Wealth is the ability to fully experience life." — Jim Rohn*

22. *"There are people who have money and people who are rich."* — Coco Chanel

23. *"The man who does more than he is paid for will soon be paid for more than he does."* — Napoleon Hill

24. *"If you want to be wealthy, study wealth."* — Robert Kiyosaki

25. *"Invest in yourself. Your career is the engine of your wealth."* — Paul Clitheroe

26. *"Money is not everything, but everything requires money."* — Unknown

27. *"The difference between a rich man and a poor man is the way they use their time."* — Robert Kiyosaki

28. *"To acquire wealth is difficult; to preserve it more difficult; but to spend it wisely most difficult of all."* — Edward Bulwer-Lytton

29. *"Wealth is not about having possessions, but about having power over them."* — David Schnarch

30. *"Wealth is the ability to fully experience life."* — Henry David Thoreau

31. *"Happiness is not in the mere possession of money; it lies in the joy of achievement, in the thrill of creative effort."* — Franklin D. Roosevelt

32. *"The rich invest in time, the poor invest in money."* — Warren Buffett

33. *"Wealth consists not in having great possessions, but in having few wants."* — Epictetus

34. *"The gratification of wealth is not found in mere possession or lavish expenditure, but in its wise application."* — Miguel de Cervantes

35. *"If you want to know what a man is really like, take notice of how he acts when he loses money." — Simone Weil*

36. *"Buy when everyone else is selling and hold until everyone else is buying. That's not just a catchy slogan. It's the very essence of successful investing." — J. Paul*

37. *"Every time you borrow money, you're robbing your future self." — Nathan W. Morris*

38. *"Empty pockets never held anyone back. Only empty heads and empty hearts can do that." — Norman Vincent Peale*

39. *"You must gain control over your money or the lack of it will forever control you." — Dave Ramsey*

40. *"Excuse me while I save, invest, and build wealth." — Stephanie Lahart*

41. *"Having talents, brains, or coming from a wealthy family does not guarantee you a rich life." — M. J. Mackenzie*

42. *"Poor people have big TVs. Rich people have big libraries." — Jim Rohn*

43. *"It is health that is real wealth and not pieces of gold or silver." — Mahatma Gandhi*

44. *"We are rich only if we control our wealth. If our wealth controls us, we are poor." — M. K. Soni*

45. *"How many millionaires do you know who have become wealthy by investing in savings accounts? I rest my case." — Robert G. Allen*

46. *"An investment in knowledge pays the best dividends." — Benjamin Franklin*

47. *"Every day is a bank account, and time is our currency. No one is rich, no one is poor, we've got 24 hours each." — Christopher Rice*

48. *"Without a rich heart, wealth is an ugly beggar." — Ralph Waldo Emerson*

49. *"It's how you deal with failure that determines how you achieve success." — David Feherty*

50. *"Too many people spend money; they earn to buy things they don't want and to impress people that they don't like." — Will Rogers*

51. *"If you have trouble imagining a 20% loss in the stock market, you shouldn't be in stocks." — John Bogle*

52. *"There is only one true wealth in all the universe — living time." — Frank Herbert*

53. *"The lack of money is the root of all evil." — Mark Twain & George Bernard*

54. *"Time is more valuable than money. You can get more money, but you cannot get more time." — Jim Rohn*

55. *"People who actually have money don't want to talk about it. They want to talk about everything else." — Curtis Jackson*

56. *"People who earn money soon become circumspect about talking about it among those who don't, largely because if they talk about it, others will demand a share, often putting strain on relationships." — James Suzman*

57. *"Money can't buy friends, but it can get you a better class of enemy." — Spike Milligan*

58. *"Never spend your money before you have earned it." — Thomas Jefferson*

59. *"It's good to have money and the things that money can buy, but it's good, too, to check up once in a while and make*

sure that you haven't lost the things that money can't buy." — George Lorimer

60. *"Money often costs too much." — Ralph Waldo Emerson*

61. *"The best way to predict your future is to create it." — Peter Drucker*

62. *"Money is a terrible master but an excellent servant." — P.T. Barnum*

63. *"A budget tells us what we can't afford, but it doesn't keep us from buying it." — William Feather*

64. *"It's not your salary that makes you rich, it's your spending habits." — Charles A. Jaffe*

65. *"Money is a poor man's credit card." — Marshall McLuhan*